OLD MOORE'S

HOROSCOPE AND ASTRAL DIARY

CAPRICORN

OLD MOORE'S

HOROSCOPE AND ASTRAL DIARY

CAPRICORN

foulsham
LONDON • NEW YORK • TORONTO • SYDNEY

foulsham

The Oriel, Thames Valley Court, 183–187 Bath Road, Slough, Berkshire SL1 4AA, England

Foulsham books can be found in all good bookshops or direct from www.foulsham.com

ISBN: 978-0-572-03611-9

Printed in Great Britain by J F Print Ltd., Sparkford, Somerset.

CONTENTS

INTRODUCTION

Welcome to *Old Moore's Astral Diary* for the year 2011. Astrology has been a part of life for centuries now, and no matter how technological our lives become, it seems that it never diminishes in popularity. For thousands of years people have been gazing up at the star-clad heavens and seeing their own activities and proclivities reflected in the movement of those little points of light. Across the centuries, countless hours have been spent studying the way our natures, activities and decisions seem to be paralleled by their predictable movements. Old Moore, a time-served veteran of astrological research, continues to monitor the zodiac and has produced the Astral Diary for 2011, tailor-made to your own astrological make-up.

Old Moore's Astral Diary is unique in its ability to get to the heart of your nature and to offer you the sort of advice that might come from a trusted friend. The Astral Diary is structured in such a way that you can see in a day-by-day sense exactly how the planets are working for you. The diary section advises how you can get the best from upcoming situations and allows you to plan ahead successfully. There is room in the daily sections to put your own observations or even appointments, and the book is conveniently structured to stay with you throughout the year.

While other popular astrology books merely deal with your astrological Sun sign, the Astral Diary goes much further. Every person on the planet is unique, and Old Moore allows you to access your individuality in a number of ways. The front section gives you the chance to work out the placement of the Moon at the time of your birth and to see how its position has set an important seal on your overall nature. Perhaps most important of all, you can use the Astral Diary to discover your Rising sign. This is the zodiac sign that was appearing over the Eastern horizon at the time of your birth and is just as important to you as an individual as is your Sun sign.

It is the synthesis of many different astrological possibilities that makes you what you are, and with the Astral Diary you can learn so much. How do you react to love and romance? Through the unique Venus tables and the readings that follow them, you can learn where the planet Venus was at the time of your birth. It is even possible to register when little Mercury is 'retrograde', which means that it appears to be moving backwards in space when viewed from the Earth. Mercury rules communication, so be prepared to deal with a few setbacks in this area when you see the sign ☿. The Astral Diary will be an interest and a support throughout the whole year ahead.

Old Moore extends his customary greeting to all people of the Earth and offers his age-old wishes for a happy and prosperous period ahead.

THE ESSENCE OF CAPRICORN

Exploring the Personality of Capricorn the Goat

(22nd DECEMBER – 20th JANUARY)

What's in a sign?

You probably think of yourself as being the least complicated person to be found anywhere. Although this is basically true, that doesn't necessarily mean that everyone understands you quite as well as they might. When faced with the real world you are practical, capable and resourceful. That means that you get on well with whatever needs to be done. Where you might sometimes fall down is in terms of communicating your intentions to the world at large – mostly it doesn't seem all that important to do so. In other words, you are not the world's best talker, and probably don't even want to be.

When it comes to sweeping away the red tape and actually getting down to the task in hand, you are second to none. Dextrous and adaptable in all matters that need your unique logic, you come at all problems with the same determination to sort them out. However, your ruling planet is cold, ponderous Saturn, and that could be where the potential problems start. Although you have a kind heart and a genuine desire to improve the lot of others, your methods are sometimes misunderstood. Some people might think you a little aloof, or even difficult to talk to. You have frequent quiet spells and often seem to be particularly content with your own company. On rare occasions this can leave you isolated.

Sharing what you are with the world at large is the most important factor on the road to a more contented life, though even this isn't certain, because most Capricorn people tend to be fairly happy with being the way they are. All the same, when those around you want to see something actually being done, they will call on you. Success is not hard for you to achieve, particularly in a career sense. You don't mind getting your hands dirty and can usually be relied upon to find ingenious answers when they are most needed.

In matters of love you are sincere and will work long and hard for your family. Romantically speaking you take some time to get going but can be ardent and sincere when you finally do. Routines don't bother you, and you can also learn to be adaptable.

Capricorn resources

You probably don't think of yourself as being the most dynamic person in the world, though you certainly are one of the most capable. When others are looking for answers, even in very practical matters, you are in there sorting things out. It's the nuts and bolts of the world that are most important, and you don't seem to have too much trouble fixing broken things – whether it's the living room chair, or the heart of a dear friend.

Instead of trying to be one of life's exciting go-getters, you are likely to be more comfortable working slowly and steadily, sometimes in the background. But this doesn't mean that you fail to make a positive impression. On the contrary, you are very necessary to those who form a part of your life, and they are ever aware of the important part you play. It isn't given to everyone to be showy and flashy, and in any case even if you forced yourself down such roads you probably wouldn't be at all comfortable in a role that doesn't come naturally to you.

One of your greatest attributes is your dry sense of humour. It's always possible for you to make others laugh, even during the most awkward or difficult situations. When the world looks particularly dark we all need a Capricorn subject along to lighten the load. You make a good colleague, know well how to co-operate and tend to work capably, either as part of a team, or when circumstances dictate, on your own.

Your greatest resource, and the one that has made many Capricorn people famous over the years, is your capacity to keep going. When there is a problem to be solved, a bridge to build, or a family to support under difficult circumstances, you really come into your own. This is probably because you don't understand the meaning of the word failure. You can find ways round any number of obstacles, and remain dependable, even when the world and his dog are falling to pieces. Add to this the fact that you are consistent and reliable and it shouldn't be too hard for you to enjoy being a capable Capricorn.

Beneath the surface

Although you might not appear to be very complicated when viewed from the perspective of those who see you on a daily basis, you are actually very complex. The reason that this is not obvious lies in the fact that you betray very little of your inner mind in your day-to-day interactions with others. In the main they see you as being capable and settled – but how wrong they can be.

The fact is that you are rarely totally sure of yourself. The confidence to get things done disguises how often you shake inside, and especially so if you are forced into the public arena. You probably wouldn't relish having to do any sort of presentation or to be put on the spot in front of individuals you consider to be more dynamic than you are. Despite this there are strong saving graces. Even when times are tough, or when you do feel a little shaky inside, your natural way forward is to keep plugging away. In some respects your zodiac sign may represent one of the bravest of them all. You won't allow yourself to be bettered by anyone, and the more pressure that is put upon you to fail, the greater is your internal desire for success.

In matters of emotion you are complicated and difficult to understand. You view relationships with the same patience that you bring to almost all facets of life. Friends can misuse or even abuse you for a while, but there is a breaking point within Capricorn that appears sudden, and very final. And once you have made up your mind to a particular course of action, there isn't any force in the world that will prevent you from implementing it.

Your natural planetary ruler is Saturn, the Lord of Time. As a result you are inclined to see things in the medium and longer term. You rarely show yourself to be impatient and carefully choose a course of action, using mental processes that usually follow tried and tested paths. You won't be hurried or pushed and will always stick to methods of working that seem to have worked for you in the past. Although this might sometimes make you feel lacking in colour or variety, you almost always get where you want to go. Occasionally your inner mind takes a great leap in logic. This can lead to a sudden change in attitude and actions that will shock the world. And why not? Even Capricorns need to keep people guessing sometimes.

You may not be the easiest person in the world to understand, or to get to know fully. Don't worry. The inner secrecy of your nature is half your appeal.

Making the best of yourself

We all need to realise what makes us tick, and to come to terms with the most comfortable way in which we can react with the world at large. This is just as true for the zodiac sign of Capricorn as it is for any other. But nobody is perfect, so what can you do to use your skills to the full and to get on better with those who share the planet with you?

Well for starters, it wouldn't be a bad idea to let others know what you are doing – and why. In practical situations especially it's sometimes much easier for you simply to get on and finish a task on your own. And despite your capabilities this is probably why you are not the world's best teacher. It's simply less complicated to get something done, and then to move on patiently to the next demand. On the way, however, you might alienate those who would love to be your friends, and to learn from you.

When it comes to emotion you should do your best to explain the way you feel. Building up animosity for days, weeks or even months, doesn't really do anyone a lot of good, not even a Capricorn subject. People can't alter to suit your needs if they don't know what it is you want. For this reason you should always be as honest as you can be, even if this proves to be quite embarrassing at first. Be willing to show your flexible side – and even to create one if necessary. Try doing things the way others want to proceed now and again, despite the fact that you could be convinced that they are wrong in their approach. Allowing those around you the right to fail is important and in the end it will only make you look that much more confident and together when you stoop to pick up the pieces.

As often as proves to be possible you should display the inner smile that burns away inside you. Be willing to let your hair down and have a good time in the company of people who really do want to know that you are happy. Most important of all, share your inner honesty with those who are important to you.

The impressions you give

There is a great disparity between the way you feel about certain situations, and the impression you offer to an unsuspecting world. If you could fully see yourself as others usually see you, it's an odds-on certainty that you would be very surprised. The vast majority of those with whom you live and work see you as being ultra confident, very cool and quite capable. If you find this hard to believe, simply ask the most honest of your friends. It doesn't matter how you feel inside, or that you often have to dig around for answers that don't supply themselves immediately. What counts is the barrier that is placed constantly between your inner mind and your outward persona.

This is very important because it means you could get on in life even better than you may appear to be doing at the moment. Think what a great gift it is rarely to show that you are quaking inside. And when your cool approach means that you find advancement coming your way, you move on to the next set of requirements with the same apparent confidence you had before.

On a less positive note, it is possible that certain of the people with whom you interact on a daily basis could find you somewhat cold and even perhaps a little aloof on occasions. This is not the case, but once again there is a screen between the way you feel and the façade you show to the world at large. And though this barrier can be your best friend, it can also be a powerful enemy, especially in emotional or romantic situations. When circumstances necessitate, it is important that you tell those with whom you share your life exactly how you feel. That allows them to modify their own behaviour to suit your needs.

There may not be a great deal of work to do on altering your approach because in the main you are well liked and certainly respected. All that is really required in any case is an understanding that what you think and the way you act are not necessarily the same thing.

The way forward

Although it's true of course that anyone can make favourable alterations to their life, it's entirely possible that yours is already headed in the right direction generally. Capricorn people are not usually too complicated; they remain modest in their objectives and can achieve their ends through the medium of good ideas and hard work. You may not give the impression of being the most exciting person in the world – and nor do you wish to be. But when it's necessary to come up with the goods, mentally and practically, you don't usually have much trouble doing so.

To be and to remain quietly confident isn't too much to ask from life. Under most circumstances you take on tasks that you know you can achieve, try to be kind to others on the way and don't tend to make too many waves. It probably doesn't bother you too much that there are people around who may not care for you. This is essentially because you are a realist and understand that you won't be everyone's cup of tea.

If there are points within your nature that could be improved with effort they might relate to a certain stubborn streak. There are occasions when you become very determined to achieve a particular objective and you may not always listen to alternatives once you think you know how to proceed. However, since you don't tend to take on tasks that you are not equipped to deal with, what some may call intransigence, you might refer to as self-assurance. It is also possible that you sometimes find it difficult to express your inner feelings, and especially those related to love. You can be somewhat suspicious of the motives of others and may guard yourself a little too carefully as a result.

Try to recognise that there is more than one way to skin a cat, and that you can actually learn and grow through co-operation. You may also need to be willing to take on a greater degree of responsibility at work, even though this might go against the grain for a whole host of reasons. When faced with decisions that have a bearing on the lives of others, seek their counsel and take note of their opinions.

There are times when you can be a little too pessimistic for your own good. It is important to cultivate a cheerful approach, even though your sometimes slightly gloomy attitude is actually revered and smiled at by your friends. You are loyal, hard-working and generally kind. Capricorn may not be the most dynamic of the zodiac signs, but it is hard to fault it all the same.

CAPRICORN ON THE CUSP

Old Moore is often asked how astrological profiles are altered for those people born at either the beginning or the end of a zodiac sign, or, more properly, on the cusps of a sign. In the case of Capricorn this would be on the 22nd of December and for two or three days after, and similarly at the end of the sign, probably from the 18th to the 20th of January. In this year's Astral Diaries, once again, Old Moore sets out to explain the differences regarding cuspid signs.

The Sagittarius Cusp – December 22nd to 24th

Oh, what a lovely person you can be, and how respected you are by the world at large. At its best this is a very fortunate combination because it retains all the practical skills of Capricorn, but the nature is somewhat elevated by the quality of Sagittarius. Nothing much is beyond your capabilities but, unlike the typical Sagittarian, you back up your words with some quite practical actions. People learn to trust you and the amount of reliance that is placed on your judgement is sometimes staggering. Of course this does infer a high degree of responsibility but this fact probably won't worry you in the slightest. From a personal point of view you are very good to know and do your best to be friendly to almost everyone. However, you don't suffer fools at all gladly and probably prefer the company of those whose thoughts and ideas run along the same sort of road as yours.

Nobody could dispute the fact that you are very reasonable but you do sometimes get so obsessed with things that you could be less accessible than Sagittarius. A little extra work may be needed in this direction, especially when you are dealing with people who don't have your fast-track approach to problems. For all this you are a deep thinker and will often weigh up the pros and cons of a particular problem if necessary. In love you are deep and sincere, but with a superficial veneer that makes you appear light, bright and fun to be with. Making your way in life isn't at all difficult and money could easily come your way. This is not a response to good luck, but to dedication and inspired hard work.

With a good combination of the practical and the inspirational, you could turn your hand to almost anything. Your confidence is usually high and you are always in a good position to get by, no matter what obstacles you encounter. You like a challenge and rarely shy away from things when the going gets tough. This is one of the reasons that others like you so much and also explains why they have such confidence in your abilities. Your sense of purpose is strong and you may be tougher than you realise.

The Aquarius Cusp – January 18th to 20th

This is the more dreamy side of Capricorn and can make for an individual who is sometimes rather difficult for others to fathom. This is hardly surprising since you don't really know your own nature quite as well as you would wish. Because the two zodiac signs are a little like oil and water you can rub along quite nicely for ages as a typical Capricorn, before suddenly shooting off at a tangent into some nether world that isn't at all like the reliable sign of the Goat. You tend to think about things fairly deeply, though with a rather 'off the wall' approach that sometimes annoys your deeper Capricorn traits. Certainly you are fascinating to know, with a magnetic personality and a basic charm that shows itself a great deal, especially when your interest is roused.

You are a lover of mystery and might appear on occasion to have a slightly dark side. This is really only a sort of morbid curiosity and it doesn't reflect your own basic nature, which is kind, sincere and anxious to please. Socially you contribute to anything that takes your fancy but you won't stay around long if you find a conversation boring. Finding the right sort of romantic partner might be somewhat difficult because you are not run-of-the-mill and have strange needs at a personal level. However, once you have set your sights in a particular direction, you stick to it. And as far as finding the right person is concerned, you could do much worse than to trust your intuition, which is strong. You don't always know what you want from life, but this fact can prove to be half of the fascination.

This unusual nature tends to fit you for occupations that demand a variety of skills, though you may change your career entirely at some stage in your life. Certainly you can be very practical, but the way things feel is important to you and you might find that you start certain tasks time and again in order to make sure that they turn out just right. This sign combination can easily lead to a desire for travel and a need to extend your personal horizons. Your restlessness is sometimes a puzzle to others, but it's a fascination, too.

CAPRICORN AND ITS ASCENDANTS

The nature of every individual on the planet is composed of the rich variety of zodiac signs and planetary positions that were present at the time of their birth. Your Sun sign, which in your case is Capricorn, is one of the many factors when it comes to assessing the unique person you are. Probably the most important consideration, other than your Sun sign, is to establish the zodiac sign that was rising over the eastern horizon at the time that you were born. This is your Ascending or Rising sign. Most popular astrology fails to take account of the Ascendant, and yet its importance remains with you from the very moment of your birth, through every day of your life. The Ascendant is evident in the way you approach the world, and so, when meeting a person for the first time, it is this astrological influence that you are most likely to notice first. Our Ascending sign essentially represents what we appear to be, while the Sun sign is what we feel inside ourselves.

The Ascendant also has the potential for modifying our overall nature. For example, if you were born at a time of day when Capricorn was passing over the eastern horizon (this would be around the time of dawn) then you would be classed as a double Capricorn. As such, you would typify this zodiac sign, both internally and in your dealings with others. However, if your Ascendant sign turned out to be an Air sign, such as Gemini, there would be a profound alteration of nature, away from the expected qualities of Capricorn.

One of the reasons why popular astrology often ignores the Ascendant is that it has always been rather difficult to establish. Old Moore has found a way to make this possible by devising an easy-to-use table, which you will find on page 159 of this book. Using this, you can establish your Ascendant sign at a glance. You will need to know your rough time of birth, then it is simply a case of following the instructions.

For those readers who have no idea of their time of birth it might be worth allowing a good friend, or perhaps your partner, to read through the section that follows this introduction. Someone who deals with you on a regular basis may easily discover your Ascending sign, even though you could have some difficulty establishing it for yourself. A good understanding of this component of your nature is essential if you want to be aware of that 'other person' who is responsible for the way you make contact with the world at large. Your Sun sign, Ascendant sign, and the other pointers in this book will, together, allow you a far better understanding of what makes you tick as an individual. Peeling back the different layers of your astrological make-up can be an enlightening experience, and the Ascendant may represent one of the most important layers of all.

Capricorn with Capricorn Ascendant

Whatever it is that you are looking for in life, there isn't much doubt that you find it. Having done so, you tend to consolidate your position before looking ahead to the next set of objectives. There isn't a more determined soul than you in the length and breadth of the whole zodiac and you will not be thwarted once you have made up your mind. It would take an astute person to pull the wool over your eyes in any practical respect, though you may not be quite so clever when it comes to the personal side of your life. You can sometimes be rather misled in love, but not if you are as determined in this direction as you are in every other sphere of life.

The most enduring quality that you possess is staying-power, and you remain certain that your long-term plans are the right ones, modifying here and tweaking there to get them just right. On the way you make few deep friends, though the ones you do have tend to stay around for years. All the same you are popular, and can attract the right sort of people to help you out. In love you are sincere and honest, a good and reliable partner, and, I am told, one of the best lovers to be found in a month of Sundays. All you need to complete the picture is a more flexible attitude.

Capricorn with Aquarius Ascendant

Here the determination of Capricorn is assisted by a slightly more adaptable quality and an off-beat personality that tends to keep everyone else guessing. You don't care to be quite so predictable as the archetypal Capricorn would be and there is a more idealistic quality, or at least one that shows more. A greater number of friends than Capricorn would usually keep is likely, though less than a true Aquarian would gather. Few people doubt your sincerity, though not all of them understand what makes you tick. Unfortunately you are not in a position to help them out, because you are not very sure yourself. All the same you muddle through and can be very capable when the mood takes you.

Being a natural traveller, you love to see new places and would be quite fascinated by cultures that are very different to your own. People with this combination are inclined to spend some time living abroad and may even settle there. You look out for the underdog and will always have time for a good cause, no matter what it takes to help. In romantic terms you are a reliable partner, though with a slightly wayward edge which, if anything, tends to make you more attractive. Listen to your intuition, which rarely lets you down. Generally speaking you are very popular.

Capricorn with Pisces Ascendant

You are certainly not the easiest person in the world to understand, mainly because your nature is so deep and your personality so complicated, that others are somewhat intimidated at the prospect of staring into this abyss. All the same your friendly nature is attractive, and there will always be people around who are fascinated by the sheer magnetic quality that is endemic to the zodiac mix. Sentimental and extremely kind, there is no limit to the extent of your efforts on behalf of a deserving world, though there are some people around who wonder at your commitment and who may ridicule you a little for your staying-power, even in the face of some adversity. At work you are very capable, will work long and hard, and can definitely expect a greater degree of financial and practical success than Pisces alone. Routines don't bother you too much, though you do need regular periods of introspection, which help to recharge low batteries and a battered self-esteem.

In affairs of the heart you are somewhat given to impulse, which belies the more careful qualities of Capricorn. However, the determination remains intact and you are quite capable of chasing rainbows around, never realising that you can't get to the end of them. You are immensely lovable and a great favourite to many.

Capricorn with Aries Ascendant

If ever anyone could be accused of setting off immediately, but slowly, it has to be you. These are very contradictory signs and the differences will express themselves in a variety of ways. One thing is certain, you have tremendous tenacity and will see a job through patiently from beginning to end, without tiring on the way, and ensuring that every detail is taken care of properly. This combination often bestows good health and a great capacity for continuity, particularly in terms of the length of life. You are certainly not as argumentative as the typical Aries, but you do know how to get your own way, which is just as well because you are usually thinking on behalf of everyone else and not just on your own account.

At home you can relax, which is a blessing for Aries, though in fact you seldom choose to do so because you always have some project or other on the go. You probably enjoy knocking down and rebuilding walls, though this is a practical tendency and not responsive to relationships, in which you are ardent and sincere. Impetuosity is as close to your heart as is the case for any type of Aries subject, though you certainly have the ability to appear patient and steady. But it's really just a front, isn't it?

Capricorn with Taurus Ascendant

It might appear on the surface that you are not the most interesting person in the world. This is a pity, for you have an active though very logical mind, so logical in some instances that you would have a great deal in common with Mr Spock. This is the thorn in your flesh, or rather the flesh of everyone else, since you are probably quite happy being exactly what you are. You can think things through in a clear and very practical way and end up taking decisions that are balanced, eminently sensible, but, on occasions, rather dull.

Actually there is a fun machine somewhere deep within that Earth-sign nature and those who know you the best will recognise the fact. Often this combination is attended by a deep and biting sense of humour, but it's of the sort that less intelligent and considered types would find rather difficult to recognise. It is likely that you have no lack of confidence in your own judgement, and you have all the attributes necessary to do very well on the financial front. Slow and steady progress is your way and you need to be quite certain before you commit yourself to any new venture. This is a zodiac combination that can soak up years of stress and numerous difficulties and yet still come out on top. Nothing holds you back for long and you tend to be very brave.

Capricorn with Gemini Ascendant

A very careful and considered combination is evident here. You still have the friendly and chatty qualities of Gemini, though you also possess an astute, clever and deep-thinking quality which can really add bite to the Mercurial aspects of your nature. Although you rarely seem to take yourself or anyone else too seriously, in reality you are not easily fooled and usually know the direction in which you are heading. The practical application of your thought processes matter to you and you always give of your best, especially in any professional situation. This combination provides the very best business mind that any Gemini could have and, unlike other versions of the sign, you are willing to allow matters to mature. This quality cannot be overstated and leads to a form of ultimate achievement that many other Geminis would only guess at.

Family matters are important to you and your home is a special place of retreat, even though you are also willing to get out and meet the world, which is the prerogative of all Gemini types. There are times when you genuinely wish to remain quiet, and when such times arise you may need to explain the situation to some of the bemused people surrounding you. Above all you look towards material gain, though without ever losing your sense of humour.

Capricorn with Cancer Ascendant

The single most important factor here is the practical ability to get things done and to see any task, professional or personal, through to the end. Since half this combination is Cancer that also means expounding much of your energy on behalf of others. There isn't a charity in the world that would fail to recognise what a potent combination this is when it comes to the very concrete side of offering help and assistance. Many of your ideas hold water and you don't set off on abortive journeys of any kind, simply because you tend to get the ground rules fixed in your mind first.

On a more personal level you can be rather hard to get to know, because both these signs have a deep quality and a tendency to keep things in the dark. The mystery may only serve to encourage people to try and get to know you better. As a result you could attract a host of admirers, many of whom would wish to form romantic attachments. This may prove to be irrelevant however, because once you give your heart, you tend to be loyal and would only change your mind if you were pushed into doing so. Prolonged periods of inactivity don't do you any good and it is sensible for you to keep on the move, even though your progress in life is measured and very steady.

Capricorn with Leo Ascendant

What really sets you apart is your endless patience and your determination to get where you want to go, no matter how long it takes you to do so. On the way there are many sub-plots in your life and a wealth of entertaining situations to keep you amused. Probably somewhat quieter than the average Leo, you still have the capacity to be the life and soul of the party on those occasions when it suits you to be so. Energy, when allied to persistence, is a powerful commodity and you have a great need to take on causes of one sort or another. Probably at your best when defending the rights of the oppressed, you take the protecting qualities of Leo to greater heights than almost anyone else touched by the idealistic and regal qualities of the sign. If arguments come into your life, you deal with them quickly and, in the main, wisely. Like most Capricorn types you take to a few individuals, who will play a part in your life for years on end.

Being a good family type, your partner and children are very important and you will lavish the same patience, determination and ultimate success on their behalf that you do when dealing with more remote situations. The fact is that you do not know any other way to behave, and you are at your best when there is a mountain to climb.

Capricorn with Virgo Ascendant

Your endurance, persistence and concentration are legendary, and there is virtually nothing that eludes you once you have the bit between your teeth. You are not the pushy, fussy, go-getting sort of Virgoan but are steady, methodical and very careful. Once you have made up your mind, a whole team of wild horses could not change it, and although this can be a distinct blessing at times, it is a quality that can bring odd problems into your life too. The difficulty starts when you adopt a lost or less than sensible cause. Even in the face of overwhelming negative evidence, there is something inside you that prevents any sort of U-turn and so you carry on as solidly as only you can, to a destination that won't suit you at all.

There are few people around who are more loyal and constant than you can be. There is a lighter and brighter side to your nature, and the one or two people who are most important in your life will know how to bring it out. You have a wicked sense of humour, particularly if you have had a drink or when you are feeling on top form. Travel does you the world of good, even if there is a part of you that would rather stay at home. You have a potent, powerful and magnetic personality, but for much of the time it is kept carefully hidden.

Capricorn with Libra Ascendant

It is a fact that Libra is the most patient of the Air signs, though like the others it needs to get things done fairly quickly. Capricorn, on the other hand, will work long and hard to achieve its objectives and will not be thwarted. As a result this is a powerful combination and one that leads ultimately to success.

Capricorn is often accused of taking itself too seriously, and yet it has an ironic and really very funny sense of humour which only its chief confidants recognise. Libra is lighthearted, always willing to have fun and quite anxious to please. When these two basic types come together in their best forms, you might find yourself to be one of the most well-balanced people around. Certainly you know what you want, but don't have to use a bulldozer in order to get it.

Active and enthusiastic when something really takes your fancy, you might also turn out to be one of the very best lovers of them all. The reason for this is that you have the depth of Capricorn but the lighter and more directly affectionate qualities of the Scales. What you want from life in a personal sense, you eventually tend to get, but you don't care too much if this takes you a while. Few people could deny that you are a faithful friend, a happy sort and a deeply magnetic personality.

Capricorn with Scorpio Ascendant

If patience, perseverance and a solid ability to get where you want to go are considered to be the chief components of a happy life, then you should be skipping about every day. Unfortunately this is not always the case, and here we have two zodiac signs who can both be too deep for their own good. Both Scorpio and Capricorn are inclined to take themselves rather too seriously, and your main lesson in life, and some would say the reason you have adopted this zodiac combination, is to 'lighten up'. If all that determination is pushed in the direction of your service to the world at large, you are seen as being one of the kindest people imaginable. This is really the only option for you, because if you turn this tremendous potential power inwards all the time you will become brooding, secretive and sometimes even selfish. Your eyes should be turned towards a needy humanity, which can be served with the dry but definite wit of Capricorn and the true compassion of Scorpio.

It is impossible with this combination to indicate what areas of life suit you the best. Certainly you adore luxury in all its forms, and yet you can get by with almost nothing. You desire travel, and at the same time love the comforts and stability of home. The people who know you best are aware that you are rather special. Listen to what they say.

Capricorn with Sagittarius Ascendant

The typical Sagittarian nature is modified for the better when Capricorn is part of the deal. It's true that you manage to push forward progressively under most circumstances, but you also possess staying power and can work long and hard to achieve your objectives, most of which are carefully planned in advance. Few people have the true measure of your nature, for it runs rather deeper than appears to be the case on the surface. Routines don't bother you as much as would be the case for Sagittarius when taken alone, and you don't care if any objective takes weeks, months or even years to achieve. You are very fond of those you take to and would certainly prove to be a capable friend, even when things get quite tough.

In love relationships you are steadfast and reliable, and yet you never lose the ability to entertain. Yours is a dry sense of humour which shows itself to a multitude of different people and which doesn't run out, even on those occasions when life gets tough. It might take you a long time to find the love of your life, but when you do there is a greater possibility of retaining the relationship for a long period. You don't tend to inherit money, but you can easily make it for yourself, though you won't worry too much about the amount. On the whole you are a very self-sufficient and sensible individual.

THE MOON AND THE PART IT PLAYS IN YOUR LIFE

In astrology the Moon is probably the single most important heavenly body after the Sun. Its unique position, as partner to the Earth on its journey around the solar system, means that the Moon appears to pass through the signs of the zodiac extremely quickly. The zodiac position of the Moon at the time of your birth plays a great part in personal character and is especially significant in the build-up of your emotional nature.

Sun Moon Cycles

The first lunar cycle deals with the part the position of the Moon plays relative to your Sun sign. I have made the fluctuations of this pattern easy for you to understand by means of a simple cyclic graph. It appears on the first page of each 'Your Month At A Glance', under the title 'Highs and Lows'. The graph displays the lunar cycle and you will soon learn to understand how its movements have a bearing on your level of energy and your abilities.

Your Own Moon Sign

Discovering the position of the Moon at the time of your birth has always been notoriously difficult because tracking the complex zodiac positions of the Moon is not easy. This process has been reduced to three simple stages with Old Moore's unique Lunar Tables. A breakdown of the Moon's zodiac positions can be found from page 25 onwards, so that once you know what your Moon Sign is, you can see what part this plays in the overall build-up of your personal character.

If you follow the instructions on the next page you will soon be able to work out exactly what zodiac sign the Moon occupied on the day that you were born and you can then go on to compare the reading for this position with those of your Sun sign and your Ascendant. It is partly the comparison between these three important positions that goes towards making you the unique individual you are.

HOW TO DISCOVER YOUR MOON SIGN

This is a three-stage process. You may need a pen and a piece of paper but if you follow the instructions below the process should only take a minute or so.

STAGE 1 First of all you need to know the Moon Age at the time of your birth. If you look at Moon Table 1, on page 23, you will find all the years between 1913 and 2011 down the left side. Find the year of your birth and then trace across to the right to the month of your birth. Where the two intersect you will find a number. This is the date of the New Moon in the month that you were born. You now need to count forward the number of days between the New Moon and your own birthday. For example, if the New Moon in the month of your birth was shown as being the 6th and you were born on the 20th, your Moon Age Day would be 14. If the New Moon in the month of your birth came after your birthday, you need to count forward from the New Moon in the previous month, which, if you were born in January, means you must look at December in the previous year. You cannot count from December in the year of your birth, as that month is *after* your birth. Whatever the result, jot this number down so that you do not forget it.

STAGE 2 Take a look at Moon Table 2 on page 24. Down the left hand column look for the date of your birth. Now trace across to the month of your birth. Where the two meet you will find a letter. Copy this letter down alongside your Moon Age Day.

STAGE 3 Moon Table 3 on page 24 will supply you with the zodiac sign the Moon occupied on the day of your birth. Look for your Moon Age Day down the left hand column and then for the letter you found in Stage 2. Where the two converge you will find a zodiac sign and this is the sign occupied by the Moon on the day that you were born.

Your Zodiac Moon Sign Explained

You will find a profile of all zodiac Moon Signs on pages 25 to 28, showing in yet another way how astrology helps to make you into the individual that you are. In each daily entry of the Astral Diary you can find the zodiac position of the Moon for every day of the year. This also allows you to discover your lunar birthdays. Since the Moon passes through all the signs of the zodiac in about a month, you can expect something like twelve lunar birthdays each year. At these times you are likely to be emotionally steady and able to make the sort of decisions that have real, lasting value.

MOON TABLE 1

YEAR	NOV	DEC	JAN	YEAR	NOV	DEC	JAN	YEAR	NOV	DEC	JAN
1913	28	27	7	1946	23	23	3	1979	19	18	27
1914	17	17	25	1947	12	12	21	1980	8	7	16
1915	7	6	15	1948	1	1/30	11	1981	26	26	6
1916	26	25	5	1949	20	19	29	1982	15	15	25
1917	14	13	24	1950	9	9	18	1983	4	4	14
1918	3	2	12	1951	29	28	7	1984	22	22	3
1919	22	21	1/31	1952	17	17	26	1985	12	12	21
1920	10	10	20	1953	6	6	15	1986	2	1/30	10
1921	29	29	9	1954	25	25	5	1987	21	20	29
1922	19	18	27	1955	14	14	24	1988	9	9	19
1923	8	8	17	1956	2	2	13	1989	28	28	7
1924	26	26	6	1957	21	21	1/30	1990	17	17	26
1925	16	15	24	1958	11	10	19	1991	6	6	15
1926	5	5	14	1959	30	29	9	1992	24	24	4
1927	24	24	3	1960	19	18	27	1993	14	14	22
1928	12	12	21	1961	8	7	16	1994	3	2	11
1929	1	1/30	11	1962	27	26	6	1995	22	22	1
1930	20	19	29	1963	15	15	25	1996	11	10	20
1931	9	9	18	1964	4	4	14	1997	30	29	9
1932	27	27	7	1965	22	22	3	1998	19	18	28
1933	17	17	25	1966	12	12	21	1999	8	7	17
1934	7	6	15	1967	2	1/30	10	2000	27	25	6
1935	26	25	5	1968	21	20	29	2001	16	15	24
1936	14	13	24	1969	9	9	19	2002	4	4	13
1937	3	2	12	1970	29	28	7	2003	24	23	3
1938	22	21	1/31	1971	18	17	26	2004	11	11	21
1939	11	10	20	1972	6	6	15	2005	1	1	10
1940	29	28	9	1973	25	25	5	2006	20	20	29
1941	19	18	27	1974	14	14	24	2007	9	9	18
1942	8	8	16	1975	3	3	12	2008	28	27	8
1943	27	27	6	1976	21	21	1/31	2009	17	16	26
1944	15	15	25	1977	11	10	19	2010	6	6	15
1945	4	4	14	1978	30	29	9	2011	25	25	4

DAY	DEC	JAN
1	i	A
2	i	A
3	m	A
4	m	A
5	n	A
6	n	A
7	n	A
8	n	A
9	n	A
10	n	A
11	n	B
12	n	B
13	n	B
14	n	B
15	n	B
16	n	B
17	n	B
18	n	B
19	n	B
20	n	B
21	n	C
22	n	C
23	q	C
24	q	C
25	q	C
26	q	C
27	q	C
28	q	C
29	q	C
30	q	C
31	q	C

M/D	i	m	n	q	A	B	C
0	SA	SA	SA	CP	CP	AQ	AQ
1	SA	SA	CP	CP	AQ	AQ	AQ
2	CP	CP	CP	AQ	AQ	AQ	PI
3	CP	CP	AQ	AQ	AQ	PI	PI
4	CP	AQ	AQ	PI	PI	PI	AR
5	AQ	AQ	PI	PI	PI	AR	AR
6	AQ	AQ	PI	AR	AR	AR	AR
7	PI	PI	AR	AR	AR	AR	TA
8	PI	PI	AR	AR	AR	TA	TA
9	AR	AR	TA	TA	TA	TA	GE
10	AR	AR	TA	TA	TA	GE	GE
11	TA	TA	TA	GE	GE	GE	GE
12	TA	TA	GE	GE	GE	GE	CA
13	GE	GE	GE	GE	GE	CA	CA
14	GE	GE	CA	CA	CA	CA	LE
15	GE	GE	GE	CA	CA	LE	LE
16	GE	CA	CA	CA	LE	LE	LE
17	CA	CA	CA	LE	LE	LE	VI
18	CA	CA	LE	LE	LE	VI	VI
19	CA	LE	LE	LE	VI	VI	VI
20	LE	LE	LE	VI	VI	LI	LI
21	LE	LE	VI	VI	LI	LI	LI
22	VI	VI	VI	LI	LI	LI	SC
23	VI	VI	VI	LI	LI	SC	SC
24	VI	VI	LI	LI	SC	SC	SC
25	LI	LI	LI	SC	SC	SA	SA
26	LI	LI	SC	SC	SA	SA	SA
27	SC	SC	SC	SA	SA	SA	CP
28	SC	SC	SC	SA	SA	CP	CP
29	SC	SA	SA	SA	CP	CP	CP

AR = Aries, TA = Taurus, GE = Gemini, CA = Cancer, LE = Leo, VI = Virgo, LI = Libra, SC = Scorpio, SA = Sagittarius, CP = Capricorn, AQ = Aquarius, PI = Pisces

MOON SIGNS

Moon in Aries

You have a strong imagination, courage, determination and a desire to do things in your own way and forge your own path through life.

Originality is a key attribute; you are seldom stuck for ideas although your mind is changeable and you could take the time to focus on individual tasks. Often quick-tempered, you take orders from few people and live life at a fast pace. Avoid health problems by taking regular time out for rest and relaxation.

Emotionally, it is important that you talk to those you are closest to and work out your true feelings. Once you discover that people are there to help, there is less necessity for you to do everything yourself.

Moon in Taurus

The Moon in Taurus gives you a courteous and friendly manner, which means you are likely to have many friends.

The good things in life mean a lot to you, as Taurus is an Earth sign that delights in experiences which please the senses. Hence you are probably a lover of good food and drink, which may in turn mean you need to keep an eye on the bathroom scales, especially as looking good is also important to you.

Emotionally you are fairly stable and you stick by your own standards. Taureans do not respond well to change. Intuition also plays an important part in your life.

Moon in Gemini

You have a warm-hearted character, sympathetic and eager to help others. At times reserved, you can also be articulate and chatty: this is part of the paradox of Gemini, which always brings duplicity to the nature. You are interested in current affairs, have a good intellect, and are good company and likely to have many friends. Most of your friends have a high opinion of you and would be ready to defend you should the need arise. However, this is usually unnecessary, as you are quite capable of defending yourself in any verbal confrontation.

Travel is important to your inquisitive mind and you find intellectual stimulus in mixing with people from different cultures. You also gain much from reading, writing and the arts but you do need plenty of rest and relaxation in order to avoid fatigue.

Moon in Cancer

The Moon in Cancer at the time of birth is a fortunate position as Cancer is the Moon's natural home. This means that the qualities of compassion and understanding given by the Moon are especially enhanced in your nature, and you are friendly and sociable and cope well with emotional pressures. You cherish home and family life, and happily do the domestic tasks. Your surroundings are important to you and you hate squalor and filth. You are likely to have a love of music and poetry.

Your basic character, although at times changeable like the Moon itself, depends on symmetry. You aim to make your surroundings comfortable and harmonious, for yourself and those close to you.

Moon in Leo

The best qualities of the Moon and Leo come together to make you warm-hearted, fair, ambitious and self-confident. With good organisational abilities, you invariably rise to a position of responsibility in your chosen career. This is fortunate as you don't enjoy being an 'also-ran' and would rather be an important part of a small organisation than a menial in a large one.

You should be lucky in love, and happy, provided you put in the effort to make a comfortable home for yourself and those close to you. It is likely that you will have a love of pleasure, sport, music and literature. Life brings you many rewards, most of them as a direct result of your own efforts, although you may be luckier than average and ready to make the best of any situation.

Moon in Virgo

You are endowed with good mental abilities and a keen receptive memory, but you are never ostentatious or pretentious. Naturally quite reserved, you still have many friends, especially of the opposite sex. Marital relationships must be discussed carefully and worked at so that they remain harmonious, as personal attachments can be a problem if you do not give them your full attention.

Talented and persevering, you possess artistic qualities and are a good homemaker. Earning your honours through genuine merit, you work long and hard towards your objectives but show little pride in your achievements. Many short journeys will be undertaken in your life.

Moon in Libra

With the Moon in Libra you are naturally popular and make friends easily. People like you, probably more than you realise, you bring fun to a party and are a natural diplomat. For all its good points, Libra is not the most stable of astrological signs and, as a result, your emotions can be a little unstable too. Therefore, although the Moon in Libra is said to be good for love and marriage, your Sun sign and Rising sign will have an important effect on your emotional and loving qualities.

You must remember to relate to others in your decision-making. Co-operation is crucial because Libra represents the 'balance' of life that can only be achieved through harmonious relationships. Conformity is not easy for you because Libra, an Air sign, likes its independence.

Moon in Scorpio

Some people might call you pushy. In fact, all you really want to do is to live life to the full and protect yourself and your family from the pressures of life. Take care to avoid giving the impression of being sarcastic or impulsive and use your energies wisely and constructively.

You have great courage and you invariably achieve your goals by force of personality and sheer effort. You are fond of mystery and are good at predicting the outcome of situations and events. Travel experiences can be beneficial to you.

You may experience problems if you do not take time to examine your motives in a relationship, and also if you allow jealousy, always a feature of Scorpio, to cloud your judgement.

Moon in Sagittarius

The Moon in Sagittarius helps to make you a generous individual with humanitarian qualities and a kind heart. Restlessness may be intrinsic as your mind is seldom still. Perhaps because of this, you have a need for change that could lead you to several major moves during your adult life. You are not afraid to stand your ground when you know your judgement is right, you speak directly and have good intuition.

At work you are quick, efficient and versatile and so you make an ideal employee. You need work to be intellectually demanding and do not enjoy tedious routines.

In relationships, you anger quickly if faced with stupidity or deception, though you are just as quick to forgive and forget. Emotionally, there are times when your heart rules your head.

Moon in Capricorn

The Moon in Capricorn makes you popular and likely to come into the public eye in some way. The watery Moon is not entirely comfortable in the Earth sign of Capricorn and this may lead to some difficulties in the early years of life. An initial lack of creative ability and indecision must be overcome before the true qualities of patience and perseverance inherent in Capricorn can show through.

You have good administrative ability and are a capable worker, and if you are careful you can accumulate wealth. But you must be cautious and take professional advice in partnerships, as you are open to deception. You may be interested in social or welfare work, which suit your organisational skills and sympathy for others.

Moon in Aquarius

The Moon in Aquarius makes you an active and agreeable person with a friendly, easy-going nature. Sympathetic to the needs of others, you flourish in a laid-back atmosphere. You are broad-minded, fair and open to suggestion, although sometimes you have an unconventional quality which others can find hard to understand.

You are interested in the strange and curious, and in old articles and places. You enjoy trips to these places and gain much from them. Political, scientific and educational work interests you and you might choose a career in science or technology.

Money-wise, you make gains through innovation and concentration and Lunar Aquarians often tackle more than one job at a time. In love you are kind and honest.

Moon in Pisces

You have a kind, sympathetic nature, somewhat retiring at times, but you always take account of others' feelings and help when you can.

Personal relationships may be problematic, but as life goes on you can learn from your experiences and develop a better understanding of yourself and the world around you.

You have a fondness for travel, appreciate beauty and harmony and hate disorder and strife. You may be fond of literature and would make a good writer or speaker yourself. You have a creative imagination and may come across as an incurable romantic. You have strong intuition, maybe bordering on a mediumistic quality, which sets you apart from the mass. You may not be rich in cash terms, but your personal gifts are worth more than gold.

CAPRICORN IN LOVE

Discover how compatible in love you are with people from the same and other signs of the zodiac. Five stars equals a match made in heaven!

Capricorn meets Capricorn

One of the best combinations because Capricorn knows what it wants and likes its partner to be the same. This may not be the deepest or most passionate of relationships, but Capricorn is adaptable enough to accept that. Material success is likely for this couple as they share the ability to move slowly towards even distant horizons. There will be words of love and a generally happy family atmosphere, and although at times the relationship may look lukewarm, it will usually remain strong and secure. Star rating: *****

Capricorn meets Aquarius

Probably one of the least likely combinations as Capricorn and Aquarius are unlikely to choose each other in the first place, unless one side is quite untypical of their sign. Capricorn approaches things in a practical way and likes to get things done, while Aquarius works almost exclusively for the moment and relies heavily on intuition. Their attitudes to romance are also diametrically opposed: Aquarius' moods tend to swing from red hot to ice cold in a minute, which is alien to steady Capricorn. Star rating: **

Capricorn meets Pisces

There is some chance of a happy relationship here, but it will need work on both sides. Capricorn is a go-getter, but likes to plan long term. Pisces is naturally more immediate, but has enough intuition to understand the Goat's thinking. Both have patience, but it will usually be Pisces who chooses to play second fiddle. The quiet nature of both signs might be a problem, as someone will have to lead, especially in social situations. Both signs should recognise this fact and accommodate it. Star rating: ***

Capricorn meets Aries

Capricorn works conscientiously to achieve its objectives and so can be the perfect companion for Aries. The Ram knows how to achieve but not how to consolidate, so the two signs have a great deal to offer one another practically. There may not be fireworks and it's sometimes doubtful how well they know each other, but it may not matter. Aries is outwardly hot but inwardly cool, whilst Capricorn can appear low-key but be a furnace underneath. Such a pairing can gradually find contentment, though both parties may wonder how this is so. Star rating: ****

Capricorn meets Taurus

If not quite a match made in heaven, this comes close. Both signs are Earthy in nature and that is a promising start. Capricorn is very practical and can make a Taurean's dreams come true. Both are tidy, like to know what is going to happen in a day-to-day sense, and are steady and committed. Taurus loves refinement, which Capricorn accepts and even helps to create. A good prognosis for material success rounds off a relationship that could easily stay the course. The only thing missing is a genuine sense of humour. Star rating: *****

Capricorn meets Gemini

Gemini has a natural fondness for Capricorn, which at first may be mutual. However, Capricorn is very organised, practical and persevering, and always achieves its goals in the end. Gemini starts out like this, but then starts to use a more instinctive and evolutionary approach, which may interfere with mutual objectives. To compensate, Gemini helps Capricorn avoid taking itself too seriously, while Capricorn brings a degree of stability into Gemini's world. When this pairing does work, though, it will be spectacular! Star rating: ***

Capricorn meets Cancer

Just about the only thing this pair have in common is the fact that both signs begin 'Ca'! Some signs of the zodiac are instigators and some are reactors, and both the Crab and the Goat are reactors. Consequently, they both need incentives from their partners but won't find it in each other and, with neither side taking the initiative, there's a spark missing. Cancer and Capricorn do think alike in some ways and so, if they can find their common purpose, they can be as happy as anyone. It's just rather unlikely. Star rating: **

Capricorn meets Leo

Despite promising appearances, this match often fails to take. Capricorn focuses on long-term objectives and, like Leo, is very practical. Both signs are capable of attaining success after a struggle, which, while requiring effort, gives them a mutual goal. But when life is easier, the cracks begin to show. Capricorn can be too serious for Leo, and the couple share few ideals. Leo loves luxury, Capricorn seeks austerity. Leo is warm but Capricorn seems cold and wintry in comparison. Both have many good points, but they don't seem to fire each other off properly. Star rating: **

Capricorn meets Virgo

One of the best possible combinations, because Virgo and Capricorn have an instinctive understanding. Both signs know the value of dedicated hard work and apply it equally in a relationship and other areas of life. Two of the most practical signs, nothing is beyond their ken, even if to outsiders they appear rather sterile or lacking in 'oomph'. What matters most is that the individuals are happy and with so much in common, the likelihood of mutual material success, and a shared devotion to home and family, there isn't much doubt of that. Star rating: *****

Capricorn meets Libra

Libra and Capricorn rub each other up the wrong way because their attitudes to life are so different, and although both are capable of doing something about this, in reality they probably won't. Capricorn is steady, determined and solid, while Libra is bright but sometimes superficial and not entirely reliable. They usually lack the instant spark needed to get them together in the first place, so when it does happen it is often because one of the partners is not very typical of their sign. Star rating: **

Capricorn meets Scorpio

Lack of communication is the governing factor here. Neither of this pair are renowned communicators and both need a partner to draw out their full verbal potential. Consequently, Scorpio may find Capricorn cold and unapproachable while Capricorn could find Scorpio dark and brooding. Both are naturally tidy and would keep a pristine house but great effort and a mutual goal is needed on both sides to overcome the missing spark. A good match on the financial side, but probably not an earthshattering personal encounter. Star rating: **

Capricorn meets Sagittarius

Any real problem here will stem from a lack of understanding. Capricorn is very practical and needs to be constantly on the go – though in a fairly low-key sort of way. Sagittarius is busy too, though always in a panic and invariably behind its deadlines, which will annoy organised Capricorn. Sagittarius doesn't really have the depth of nature that best suits an Earth sign like Capricorn and its flirty nature could upset the sensitive Goat, but their lighter attitude could be cheering, too. Star rating: ***

VENUS:
THE PLANET OF LOVE

If you look up at the sky around sunset or sunrise you will often see Venus in close attendance to the Sun. It is arguably one of the most beautiful sights of all and there is little wonder that historically it became associated with the goddess of love. But although Venus is important in your attitude to love and in the way others see you romantically, this is only one of its spheres of influence.

Venus plays a part in the cultured side of your life and has much to do with your appreciation of art, literature, music and general creativity. Even the way you look is responsive to the part of the zodiac that Venus occupied at the start of your life, though this is also down to your Sun sign and Ascending sign. If, at the time you were born, Venus occupied one of the more gregarious zodiac signs, you will be open in love, as well as more attracted to entertainment, social gatherings and good company. If on the other hand Venus occupied a quiet zodiac sign at the time of your birth, you would tend to be more retiring and less willing to shine in public situations.

Venus can have a great bearing on your outward appearance and since we all have to mix with others, knowledge of Venus' position at your birth can help you learn to make the best of what it has to offer you.

One of the great complications in the past has always been trying to establish exactly what zodiac position Venus enjoyed when you were born because the planet is notoriously difficult to track. Here I have created an exclusive table for your Sun sign, shown opposite.

To calculate your Venus sign, first look up the year of your birth in the table. As Capricorn naturally spans two calendar years every time it comes around, double-check that you are looking at the right line. The table is organised so that December is always the first month, so, for instance, if you were born in December 1940 or January 1941 you would look at the column for 1940–1, because the year on the calendar has changed while the zodiac is still in the sign of Capricorn. If you were born in January 1942 you would look at the column for 1941–2. Once you have the right column, you will see a sign of the zodiac next to the date. This was the sign that Venus occupied in that year. If Venus occupied more than one sign during the period, this is indicated by the date on which the sign changed and the name of the new sign. For instance, if you are looking at the years 1940–1, Venus was in Sagittarius until the 15th January, after which time it was in Capricorn. If you were born before 15th January your Venus sign is Sagittarius, if you were born on or after 15th January, your Venus sign is Capricorn. Once you have established the position of Venus at the time of your birth, you can then look in the pages which follow to see how this has a bearing on your life.

1913–14 SAGITTARIUS / 30.12 CAPRICORN
1914–15 SCORPIO / 2.1 SAGITTARIUS
1915–16 CAPRICORN / 27.12 AQUARIUS /
    20.1 PISCES
1916–17 SAGITTARIUS / 16.1 CAPRICORN
1917–18 AQUARIUS
1918–19 CAPRICORN / 10.1 AQUARIUS
1919–20 SCORPIO / 5.1 SAGITTARIUS
1920–1 AQUARIUS / 7.1 PISCES
1921–2 SAGITTARIUS / 30.12 CAPRICORN
1922–3 SCORPIO / 6.1 SAGITTARIUS
1923–4 CAPRICORN / 26.12 AQUARIUS /
    19.1 PISCES
1924–5 SAGITTARIUS / 15.1 CAPRICORN
1925–6 AQUARIUS
1926–7 CAPRICORN / 9.1 AQUARIUS
1927–8 SCORPIO / 4.1 SAGITTARIUS
1928–9 AQUARIUS / 6.1 PISCES
1929–30 SAGITTARIUS / 29.12 CAPRICORN
1930–1 SCORPIO / 3.1 SAGITTARIUS
1931–2 CAPRICORN / 26.12 AQUARIUS /
    19.1 PISCES
1932–3 SAGITTARIUS / 15.1 PISCES
1933–4 AQUARIUS
1934–5 CAPRICORN / 9.1 AQUARIUS
1935–6 SCORPIO / 4.1 SAGITTARIUS
1936–7 AQUARIUS / 6.1 PISCES
1937–8 SAGITTARIUS / 29.12 CAPRICORN
1938–9 SCORPIO / 3.1 SAGITTARIUS
1939–40 CAPRICORN / 25.12 AQUARIUS /
    18.1 PISCES
1940–1 SAGITTARIUS / 15.1 CAPRICORN
1941–2 AQUARIUS
1942–3 CAPRICORN / 8.1 AQUARIUS
1943–4 SCORPIO / 3.1 SAGITTARIUS
1944–5 AQUARIUS / 5.1 PISCES
1945–6 SAGITTARIUS / 28.12 CAPRICORN
1946–7 SCORPIO / 3.1 SAGITTARIUS
1947–8 CAPRICORN / 25.12 AQUARIUS /
    18.1 PISCES
1948–9 SAGITTARIUS / 14.1 CAPRICORN
1949–50 AQUARIUS
1950–1 CAPRICORN / 8.1 AQUARIUS
1951–2 SCORPIO / 3.1 SAGITTARIUS
1952–3 AQUARIUS / 5.1 PISCES
1953–4 SAGITTARIUS / 28.12 CAPRICORN
1954–5 SCORPIO / 4.1 SAGITTARIUS
1955–6 CAPRICORN / 24.12 AQUARIUS /
    17.1 PISCES
1956–7 SAGITTARIUS / 14.1 CAPRICORN
1957–8 AQUARIUS
1958–9 CAPRICORN / 7.1 AQUARIUS
1959–60 SCORPIO / 2.1 SAGITTARIUS
1960–1 AQUARIUS / 5.1 PISCES
1961–2 SAGITTARIUS / 28.12 CAPRICORN

1962–3 SCORPIO / 4.1 SAGITTARIUS
1963–4 CAPRICORN / 24.12 AQUARIUS /
    17.1 PISCES
1964–5 SAGITTARIUS / 13.1 CAPRICORN
1965–6 AQUARIUS
1966–7 CAPRICORN / 7.1 AQUARIUS
1967–8 SCORPIO / 2.1 SAGITTARIUS
1968–9 AQUARIUS / 5.1 PISCES
1969–70 SAGITTARIUS / 27.12 CAPRICORN
1970–1 SCORPIO / 5.1 SAGITTARIUS
1971–2 CAPRICORN / 23.12 AQUARIUS /
    16.1 PISCES
1972–3 SAGITTARIUS / 12.1 CAPRICORN
1973–4 AQUARIUS
1974–5 CAPRICORN / 6.1 AQUARIUS
1975–6 SCORPIO / 1.1 SAGITTARIUS
1976–7 AQUARIUS / 4.1 PISCES
1977–8 SAGITTARIUS / 27.12 CAPRICORN
1978–9 SCORPIO / 5.1 SAGITTARIUS
1979–80 CAPRICORN / 23.12 AQUARIUS /
    16.1 PISCES
1980–1 SAGITTARIUS / 12.1 CAPRICORN
1981–2 AQUARIUS
1982–3 CAPRICORN / 6.1 AQUARIUS
1983–4 SCORPIO / 1.1 SAGITTARIUS
1984–5 AQUARIUS / 4.1 PISCES
1985–6 SAGITTARIUS / 27.12 CAPRICORN
1986–7 SCORPIO / 6.1 SAGITTARIUS
1987–8 AQUARIUS / 15.1 PISCES
1988–9 SAGITTARIUS / 11.1 CAPRICORN
1989–90 AQUARIUS / 17.1 CAPRICORN
1990–1 CAPRICORN / 5.1 AQUARIUS
1991–2 SCORPIO / 1.1 SAGITTARIUS
1992–3 AQUARIUS / 4.1 PISCES
1993–4 SAGITTARIUS / 26.12 CAPRICORN
1994–5 SCORPIO / 7.1 SAGITTARIUS
1995–6 AQUARIUS / 15.1 PISCES
1996–7 SAGITTARIUS / 11.1 CAPRICORN
1997–8 AQUARIUS / 14.1 CAPRICORN
1998–9 CAPRICORN / 5.1 AQUARIUS
1999–2000 SCORPIO / 1.1 SAGITTARIUS
2000–01 SAGITTARIUS / 26.12 CAPRICORN
2001–02 CAPRICORN / 4.1 AQUARIUS
2002–03 SAGITTARIUS / 26.12 CAPRICORN
2003–04 SCORPIO / 7.1 SAGITTARIUS
2004–05 SAGITTARIUS / 30.12 CAPRICORN
2005–06 AQUARIUS / 2.1 CAPRICORN
2006–07 AQUARIUS / 14.1 CAPRICORN
2007–08 CAPRICORN / 5.1 AQUARIUS
2008–09 SCORPIO / 1.1 SAGITTARIUS
2009–10 SAGITTARIUS /
    26.12 CAPRICORN
2010–11 SAGITTARIUS /
    26.12 CAPRICORN
2011–12 CAPRICORN / 4.12 AQUARIUS

VENUS THROUGH THE ZODIAC SIGNS

Venus in Aries

Amongst other things, the position of Venus in Aries indicates a fondness for travel, music and all creative pursuits. Your nature tends to be affectionate and you would try not to create confusion or difficulty for others if it could be avoided. Many people with this planetary position have a great love of the theatre, and mental stimulation is of the greatest importance. Early romantic attachments are common with Venus in Aries, so it is very important to establish a genuine sense of romantic continuity. Early marriage is not recommended, especially if it is based on sympathy. You may give your heart a little too readily on occasions.

Venus in Taurus

You are capable of very deep feelings and your emotions tend to last for a very long time. This makes you a trusting partner and lover, whose constancy is second to none. In life you are precise and careful and always try to do things the right way. Although this means an ordered life, which you are comfortable with, it can also lead you to be rather too fussy for your own good. Despite your pleasant nature, you are very fixed in your opinions and quite able to speak your mind. Others are attracted to you and historical astrologers always quoted this position of Venus as being very fortunate in terms of marriage. However, if you find yourself involved in a failed relationship, it could take you a long time to trust again.

Venus in Gemini

As with all associations related to Gemini, you tend to be quite versatile, anxious for change and intelligent in your dealings with the world at large. You may gain money from more than one source but you are equally good at spending it. There is an inference here that you are a good communicator, via either the written or the spoken word, and you love to be in the company of interesting people. Always on the look-out for culture, you may also be very fond of music, and love to indulge the curious and cultured side of your nature. In romance you tend to have more than one relationship and could find yourself associated with someone who has previously been a friend or even a distant relative.

Venus in Cancer

You often stay close to home because you are very fond of family and enjoy many of your most treasured moments when you are with those you love. Being naturally sympathetic, you will always do anything you can to support those around you, even people you hardly know at all. This charitable side of your nature is your most noticeable trait and is one of the reasons why others are naturally so fond of you. Being receptive and in some cases even psychic, you can see through to the soul of most of those with whom you come into contact. You may not commence too many romantic attachments but when you do give your heart, it tends to be unconditionally.

Venus in Leo

It must become quickly obvious to almost anyone you meet that you are kind, sympathetic and yet determined enough to stand up for anyone or anything that is truly important to you. Bright and sunny, you warm the world with your natural enthusiasm and would rarely do anything to hurt those around you, or at least not intentionally. In romance you are ardent and sincere, though some may find your style just a little overpowering. Gains come through your contacts with other people and this could be especially true with regard to romance, for love and money often come hand in hand for those who were born with Venus in Leo. People claim to understand you, though you are more complex than you seem.

Venus in Virgo

Your nature could well be fairly quiet no matter what your Sun sign might be, though this fact often manifests itself as an inner peace and would not prevent you from being basically sociable. Some delays and even the odd disappointment in love cannot be ruled out with this planetary position, though it's a fact that you will usually find the happiness you look for in the end. Catapulting yourself into romantic entanglements that you know to be rather ill-advised is not sensible, and it would be better to wait before you committed yourself exclusively to any one person. It is the essence of your nature to serve the world at large and through doing so it is possible that you will attract money at some stage in your life.

Venus in Libra

Venus is very comfortable in Libra and bestows upon those people who have this planetary position a particular sort of kindness that is easy to recognise. This is a very good position for all sorts of friendships and also for romantic attachments that usually bring much joy into your life. Few individuals with Venus in Libra would avoid marriage and since you are capable of great depths of love, it is likely that you will find a contented personal life. You like to mix with people of integrity and intelligence but don't take kindly to scruffy surroundings or work that means getting your hands too dirty. Careful speculation, good business dealings and money through marriage all seem fairly likely.

Venus in Scorpio

You are quite open and tend to spend money quite freely, even on those occasions when you don't have very much. Although your intentions are always good, there are times when you get yourself in to the odd scrape and this can be particularly true when it comes to romance, which you may come to late or from a rather unexpected direction. Certainly you have the power to be happy and to make others contented on the way, but you find the odd stumbling block on your journey through life and it could seem that you have to work harder than those around you. As a result of this, you gain a much deeper understanding of the true value of personal happiness than many people ever do, and are likely to achieve true contentment in the end.

Venus in Sagittarius

You are lighthearted, cheerful and always able to see the funny side of any situation. These facts enhance your popularity, which is especially high with members of the opposite sex. You should never have to look too far to find romantic interest in your life, though it is just possible that you might be too willing to commit yourself before you are certain that the person in question is right for you. Part of the problem here extends to other areas of life too. The fact is that you like variety in everything and so can tire of situations that fail to offer it. All the same, if you choose wisely and learn to understand your restless side, then great happiness can be yours.

Venus in Capricorn

The most notable trait that comes from Venus in this position is that it makes you trustworthy and able to take on all sorts of responsibilities in life. People are instinctively fond of you and love you all the more because you are always ready to help those who are in any form of need. Social and business popularity can be yours and there is a magnetic quality to your nature that is particularly attractive in a romantic sense. Anyone who wants a partner for a lover, a spouse and a good friend too would almost certainly look in your direction. Constancy is the hallmark of your nature and unfaithfulness would go right against the grain. You might sometimes be a little too trusting.

Venus in Aquarius

This location of Venus offers a fondness for travel and a desire to try out something new at every possible opportunity. You are extremely easy to get along with and tend to have many friends from varied backgrounds, classes and inclinations. You like to live a distinct sort of life and gain a great deal from moving about, both in a career sense and with regard to your home. It is not out of the question that you could form a romantic attachment to someone who comes from far away or be attracted to a person of a distinctly artistic and original nature. What you cannot stand is jealousy, for you have friends of both sexes and would want to keep things that way.

Venus in Pisces

The first thing people tend to notice about you is your wonderful, warm smile. Being very charitable by nature you will do anything to help others, even if you don't know them well. Much of your life may be spent sorting out situations for other people, but it is very important to feel that you are living for yourself too. In the main, you remain cheerful, and tend to be quite attractive to members of the opposite sex. Where romantic attachments are concerned, you could be drawn to people who are significantly older or younger than yourself or to someone with a unique career or point of view. It might be best for you to avoid marrying whilst you are still very young.

THE ASTRAL DIARY

HOW THE DIAGRAMS WORK

Through the picture diagrams in the Astral Diary I want to help you to plot your year. With them you can see where the positive and negative aspects will be found in each month. To make the most of them, all you have to do is remember where and when!

Let me show you how they work ...

THE MONTH AT A GLANCE

Just as there are twelve separate zodiac signs, so astrologers believe that each sign has twelve separate aspects to life. Each of the twelve segments relates to a different personal aspect. I list them all every month so that their meanings are always clear.

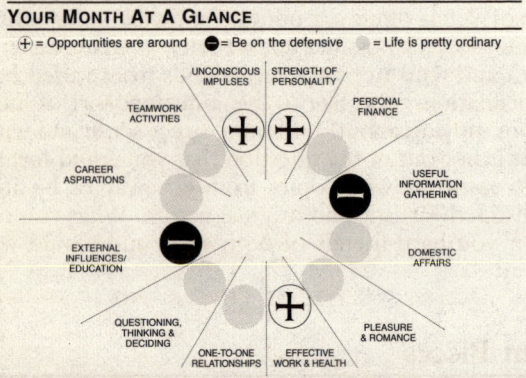

YOUR MONTH AT A GLANCE

⊕ = Opportunities are around   ● = Be on the defensive   = Life is pretty ordinary

UNCONSCIOUS IMPULSES
STRENGTH OF PERSONALITY
TEAMWORK ACTIVITIES
PERSONAL FINANCE
CAREER ASPIRATIONS
USEFUL INFORMATION GATHERING
EXTERNAL INFLUENCES/ EDUCATION
DOMESTIC AFFAIRS
QUESTIONING, THINKING & DECIDING
PLEASURE & ROMANCE
ONE-TO-ONE RELATIONSHIPS
EFFECTIVE WORK & HEALTH

I have designed this chart to show you how and when these twelve different aspects are being influenced throughout the year. When there is a shaded circle, nothing out of the ordinary is to be expected. However, when a circle turns white with a plus sign, the influence is positive. Where the circle is black with a minus sign, it is a negative.

YOUR ENERGY RHYTHM CHART

On the opposite page is a picture diagram in which I am linking your zodiac group to the rhythm of the Moon. In doing this I have calculated when you will be gaining strength from its influence and equally when you may be weakened by it.

If you think of yourself as being like the tides of the ocean then you may understand how your own energies must also rise and fall. And if you understand how it works and when it is working, then you can better organise your activities to achieve more and get things done more easily.

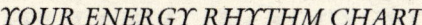

YOUR ENERGY RHYTHM CHART

Increasing in energy as the month goes on

At your best on 20th–21st

HIGH 20TH 21ST

Energy falling again from the 23rd

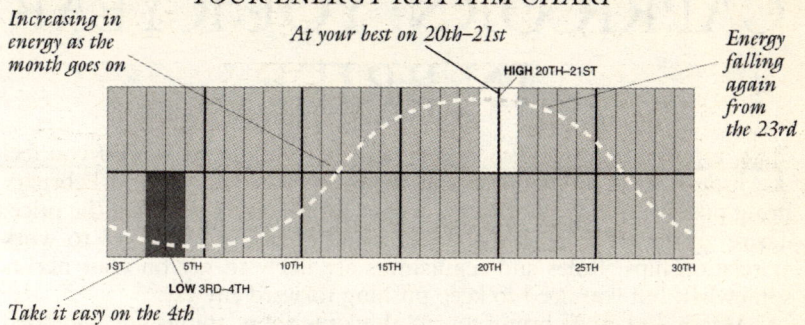

1ST 5TH 10TH 15TH 20TH 25TH 30TH

LOW 3RD–4TH

Take it easy on the 4th

MOVING PICTURE SCREEN

Love, money, career and vitality measured every week

The diagram at the end of each week is designed to be informative and fun. The arrows move up and down the scale to give you an idea of the strength of your opportunities in each area. If LOVE stands at plus 4, then get out and put yourself about because things are going your way in romance! The further down the arrow goes, the weaker the opportunities. Do note that the diagram is an overall view of your astrological aspects and therefore reflects a trend which may not concur with every day in that cycle.

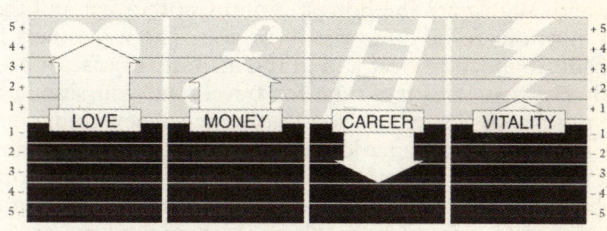

AND FINALLY:

am ....

pm ....

The two lines that are left blank in each daily entry of the Astral Diary are for your own personal use. You may find them ideal for keeping a check on birthdays or appointments, though it could be an idea to make notes from the astrological trends and diagrams a few weeks in advance. Some of the lines are marked with a key, which indicates the working of astrological cycles in your life. Look out for them each week as they are the best days to take action or make decisions. The daily text tells you which area of your life to focus on.

☿ = Mercury is retrograde on that day.

CAPRICORN: YOUR YEAR IN BRIEF

It's important to start the year as you mean to go on, even if you feel a little lacking in vitality as things get started. January and February bring positive trends and a desire to get ahead, no matter what the price. There are financial gains to be made and plenty of incentives to work at relationships. Rules and regulations are likely to get on your nerves somewhat, but you need to keep pushing forward anyway.

March and April bring you to thinking about things you intended to do, but didn't get round to. Now is as good a time as any to take opportunities as and when they arise and to incorporate them with past plans as much as proves to be possible. Don't be too picky about things and try to be especially understanding in relationships. You might need to be very supportive in terms of family.

It could seem as if the world doesn't understand you at first during May, but by June you will be back on course and anxious to get everything going the way you want. Throughout both months you have cause to look hard at relationships, and you may not be quite as sure of yourself as would sometimes be the case. Still, you know how to work hard and how to get what you want in the end – and that's what really counts.

July and August are the hottest months of the year and they should certainly turn out to be quite warm for you. The way others feel about you is made abundantly clear and in the majority of cases it proves to be extremely positive. This is a time for travel, and you should be up for any sort of journey that allows you to experience new things and faraway places. Concern for the underdog is especially highlighted during August, and you will be doing all you can for those who are less well off.

With the months of September and October comes a slight slowing of incentives and general happenings. You might have to be content with second-best on occasions, but can still put in the effort necessary to increase your personal fortune. Love shines brightly in your life and there are gains to be made from a change of job or an alteration in the emphasis of your life.

The last two months of the year, November and December, are fairly positive and work out well in terms of personal attachments and money. Don't argue for your limitations during November, but rather for your strengths. Although you will get some things wrong, in the end you will see that you are even cleverer than you thought. Christmas should be a particularly enticing period this time around, and the holidays can be a magical time for you.

January
2011

Your Month at a Glance

⊕ = Opportunities are around ⊖ = Be on the defensive ● = Life is pretty ordinary

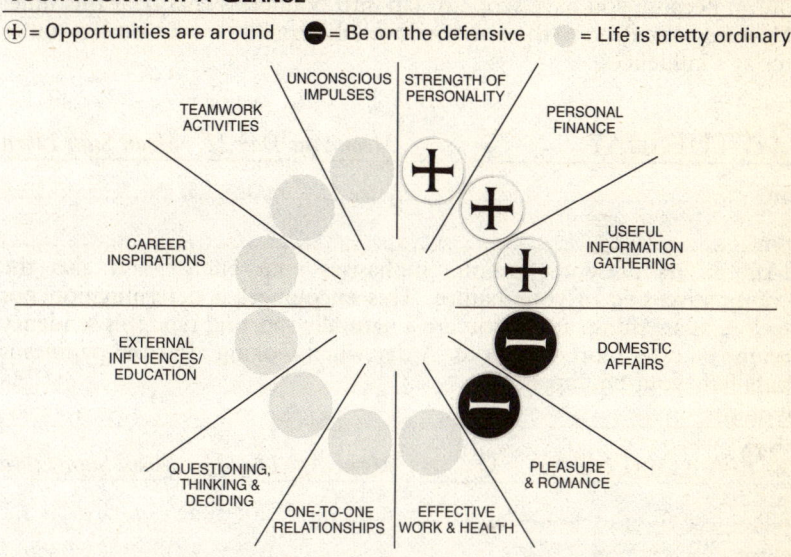

- UNCONSCIOUS IMPULSES
- STRENGTH OF PERSONALITY
- TEAMWORK ACTIVITIES
- PERSONAL FINANCE
- CAREER INSPIRATIONS
- USEFUL INFORMATION GATHERING
- EXTERNAL INFLUENCES/ EDUCATION
- DOMESTIC AFFAIRS
- QUESTIONING, THINKING & DECIDING
- PLEASURE & ROMANCE
- ONE-TO-ONE RELATIONSHIPS
- EFFECTIVE WORK & HEALTH

January Highs and Lows

Here I show you how the rhythms of the Moon will affect you this month. Like the tide, your energies and abilities will rise and fall with its pattern. When it is above the centre line, go for it, when it is below, you should be resting.

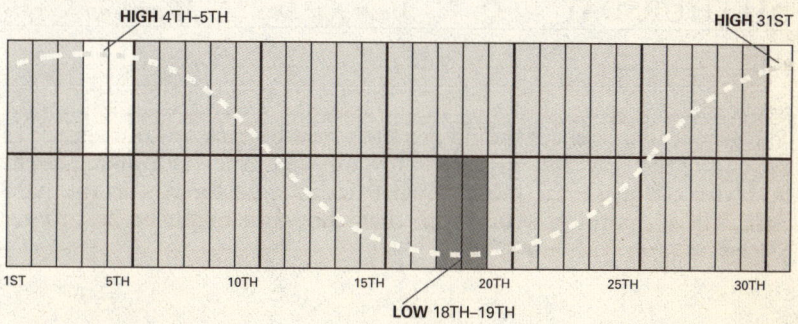

HIGH 4TH–5TH

HIGH 31ST

LOW 18TH–19TH

1ST 5TH 10TH 15TH 20TH 25TH 30TH

41

27 MONDAY ☿ *Moon Age Day 21 Moon Sign Virgo*

am ....

pm ....
It's worth making sure that everyday life has something about it that is
miles from being ordinary. It doesn't matter how much effort you have to
put in because you have scope to tap into boundless energy at this time.
Devoting attention to the one you love can certainly work wonders under
today's influences.

28 TUESDAY ☿ *Moon Age Day 22 Moon Sign Libra*

am ....

pm ....
Mars in its present position emphasises your energy and also the
competitive side of your nature. This encourages a determination not
to lose at anything, and if you are a naturally sporting type this tendency
might be even more enhanced. A day when looking after the pennies is
definitely your best approach.

29 WEDNESDAY ☿ *Moon Age Day 23 Moon Sign Libra*

am ....

pm ....
A boost to teamwork is on offer for you now, and trends encourage you
to socialise with groups rather than with individuals. You might even be
thinking about joining some sort of club or society, which would be a
positive way of taking full advantage of present planetary trends.

30 THURSDAY ☿ *Moon Age Day 24 Moon Sign Scorpio*

am ....

pm ....
The go-ahead influences should definitely now be back on your agenda as
the end of the year comes spinning towards you. Are you thinking about
how you can make the most of what lies in store for you in the New
Year? There's nothing wrong with that, though it might be best to get
December over with first of all!

31 FRIDAY
Moon Age Day 25   Moon Sign Scorpio

am...

pm...
There are good reasons to be sociable and giving for the last day of the year, and this can help you to boost your own popularity. There is much to be said for choosing to do something fairly exciting during the day, whilst you prepare yourself mentally for any festivities that are arranged for later.

1 SATURDAY
Moon Age Day 26   Moon Sign Scorpio

am...

pm...
With the improved respect you can gain from others, you can really make an impression on the first day of the year. Venus is in your solar eleventh house and this allows you to extend yourself socially. By all means look to friends for affection and remain on good form, even if you do begin the day with something of a headache!

2 SUNDAY
Moon Age Day 27   Moon Sign Sagittarius

am...

pm...
At this time of the year the Sun is in your solar first house, so this is really your time to shine. Keep your mind focused on the matter at hand and show just how capable you can be. Capricorn is a very practical zodiac sign and it really pays to show that fact significantly, not just today but across the first full week of the year, which stands in front of you.

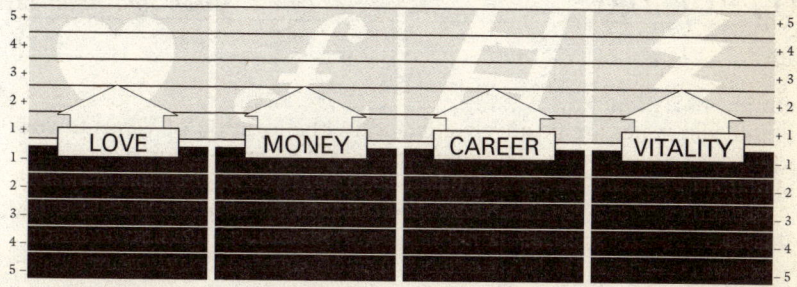

3 MONDAY
Moon Age Day 28   Moon Sign Sagittarius

am ....

pm ....

A slightly quieter day allows you to set a positive scene for what comes later. You have time to think and to plan what you want to do throughout what could be a most successful week all round. With the Moon now in your solar twelfth house you are able to mull things over carefully and to make up your mind what you will do tomorrow.

4 TUESDAY
Moon Age Day 0   Moon Sign Capricorn

am ....

pm ....

Today the Moon passes into your own zodiac sign of Capricorn and this brings the part of the month known as the lunar high. All possibilities are evident and you needn't allow much to hold you back. You can afford to keep up the pressure for advancement at work, and to find time later in the day to let down your hair alongside friends.

5 WEDNESDAY
Moon Age Day 1   Moon Sign Capricorn

am ....

pm ....

The things you achieve now have favourable influences, not simply for this month but for a long time to come. The emphasis is on starting the year in a very positive frame of mind, and this assists you to gain a great deal of ground quite quickly. By all means continue to look at things and plan in the way Capricorn always does, but you can also be very active.

6 THURSDAY
Moon Age Day 2   Moon Sign Aquarius

am ....

pm ....

Friendship issues are positively affected by the position of Venus in your solar chart around now. This encourages you to make some new friends, or even to look at existing attachments in a slightly different way. There could be lots of offers available at this time, and if there is any problem at all it comes from having to choose between them.

7 FRIDAY

Moon Age Day 3   Moon Sign Aquarius

am ....

pm...
One of the reasons you have so much energy at the moment is that Mars, in addition to the Sun, is positioned in your solar first house. When it comes to keeping up with activities of almost any sort you should be second to none, and have what it takes to be quite positive in your general attitude. However, a little snappiness can't be ruled out!

8 SATURDAY

Moon Age Day 4   Moon Sign Aquarius

am ....

pm...
This would be an ideal time to seek out a position of leadership, making sure that it comes without too much in the way of depressing responsibility. To have one without the other is quite rare, so you may as well enjoy what life is offering. The spotlight is on your determination to be quite definite in your opinions and tastes right now.

9 SUNDAY

Moon Age Day 5   Moon Sign Pisces

am ....

pm...
Trends on this particular Sunday assist you to show your sympathy and understanding. Capricorn always cares deeply for others but isn't always that good at showing the fact. Now you can offer verbal as well as physical support and can win out in the popularity stakes as a result of your actions. Today is all about helping others.

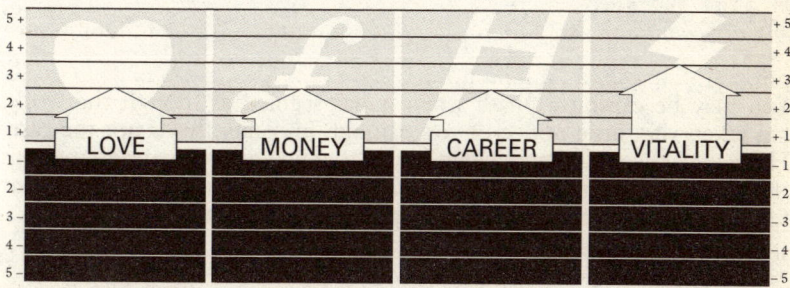

10 MONDAY *Moon Age Day 6   Moon Sign Pisces*

am ....

pm...
Think about the consequences of any new undertakings today. Mars remains in your solar first house, indicating a potentially busy time. Can you handle new projects, and do you really want to do so? You might be feeling on top form physically, but even Capricorn can push itself too hard and that would be a mistake.

11 TUESDAY *Moon Age Day 7   Moon Sign Aries*

am ....

pm...
You may now be able to bring about beneficial changes in personal affairs, and can use new ideas to pep up your romantic life no end. Why not have an evening out somewhere, especially if you are busy during the day? This will allow you to please yourself, and someone else too.

12 WEDNESDAY *Moon Age Day 8   Moon Sign Aries*

am ....

pm...
You would be wise to make sure you are as clear as possible about things before you discuss them in detail with other people. For this reason it would be worth spending an hour or two at the beginning of the day thinking things through. There is much about today that could prove to be very funny, not least of all your own reactions to situations.

13 THURSDAY *Moon Age Day 9   Moon Sign Aries*

am ....

pm...
You may be exiting a phase when it has seemed as though the world has taken very little notice of you, though in reality this is not the case. However, you should now begin to feel that you can put yourself more in the public eye in one way or another. This is not a good time to rush your fences. Slow and steady wins the Capricorn race every time.

14 FRIDAY

Moon Age Day 10   Moon Sign Taurus

am...

pm...
With a more competitive element entering your life around now, the signs are that you really do want to win – even when it isn't vital to do so. Priorities are something you need to work out early in the day, otherwise you could spend a great deal of time doing things that aren't really very important. You can afford to support a good friend today.

15 SATURDAY

Moon Age Day 11   Moon Sign Taurus

am...

pm...
Getting ahead now has a great deal to do with your level of energy and your personal determination. Mars is supporting you all the way, but it may also be pushing you slightly too hard in some respects. In most situations you might choose to work alone if at all possible, but only so that you can make sure everything is being done properly.

16 SUNDAY

Moon Age Day 12   Moon Sign Gemini

am...

pm...
Your efficiency at work shouldn't be in doubt, though of course if you don't work on a Sunday this probably doesn't have a bearing on your day. Nevertheless, it pays to keep active, and to be very enterprising in the way you are looking at life just now. Be prepared to deal with demands for attention from family members.

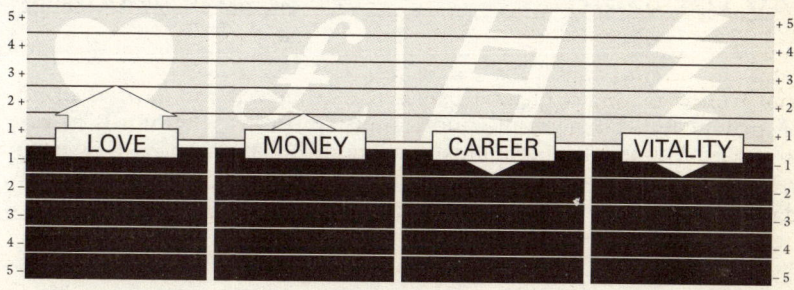

17 MONDAY *Moon Age Day 13   Moon Sign Gemini*

am ....

pm...
Your vitality and charm can now help you to increase your popularity with just about everyone, which makes for an interesting start to the week. This is a favourable time for social activities, for getting out of the house and doing something fascinating, and also for having the opportunity to do something that proves your intellectual prowess.

18 TUESDAY *Moon Age Day 14   Moon Sign Cancer*

am ....

pm...
This is the time of the month when the Moon enters your opposite zodiac sign of Cancer and it is known as the lunar low. At such times it may be difficult to summon quite as much energy, and you could feel slightly less confident than has been the case. Fortunately, you still have that first-house Mars, which offers significant support and resilience.

19 WEDNESDAY *Moon Age Day 15   Moon Sign Cancer*

am ....

pm...
Be prepared to deal with unexpected hold-ups today in terms of general progress, together with a few minor frustrations caused by other people. You may consider today that if you were left to your own devices you could achieve anything, but in reality you need support from others and would be worse off without it at this stage.

20 THURSDAY *Moon Age Day 16   Moon Sign Leo*

am ....

pm...
A new phase of dynamism is now available because the Sun is in your solar first house. This highlights how good you are to know, how happy you are to be you, and how much confidence you have in most situations. Long-term plans should now be starting to pay off and you have what it takes to impress even the most exacting of people.

21 FRIDAY
Moon Age Day 17   Moon Sign Leo

am ....

pm..
It's important to try to comprehend the emotions of others to a greater extend today – at least if you want to know why they are behaving in the way they are. Capricorn is kind and generally understanding but it is not the most perceptive of zodiac signs when it comes to analysing others. Your ability to do so is much improved now.

22 SATURDAY
Moon Age Day 18   Moon Sign Virgo

am ....

pm..
There should be plenty of comings and goings today, and many of them could involve you directly. It is possible you might decide that if you don't act, something is going to go dramatically wrong. You need to ask yourself whether this is actually the case. Try to settle down because there are strong planetary energies exerting an influence.

23 SUNDAY
Moon Age Day 19   Moon Sign Virgo

am ....

pm..
An ideal day for dealing with financial matters. Don't be afraid to stick with the decisions you have been making recently regarding your long-term fiscal future. This may not be the best time of the month to make startling changes, though if you do feel the need to reorganise any part of your life, at least let those around you know what you intend.

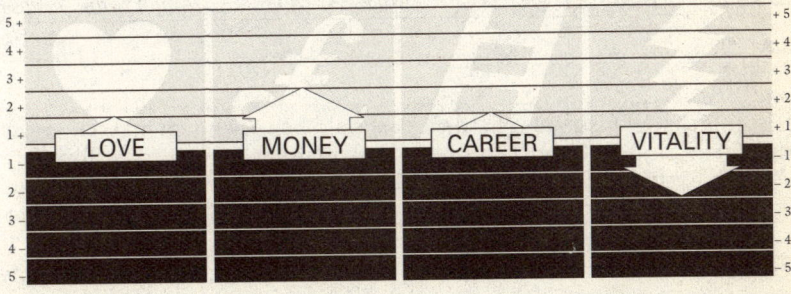

24 MONDAY
Moon Age Day 20   Moon Sign Libra

am ....

pm..
When it comes to your career there are good reasons to seek help from people in positions of authority at this time. Think carefully about how you make the approach, and how you can show them just how capable and trustworthy you are. Influencing life is always much easier under the sort of planetary influences that stand around you now.

25 TUESDAY
Moon Age Day 21   Moon Sign Libra

am ....

pm..
Venus is in your solar twelfth house, encouraging a more contemplative and even dreamy interlude when it comes to thinking about matters of the heart. You may also decide to focus on spiritual and meditative matters, which somewhat counters the more material qualities in your nature. Today is about how good you are to know, and how popular you can be!

26 WEDNESDAY
Moon Age Day 22   Moon Sign Libra

am ....

pm..
Friends can be the source of some very stimulating conversation, and there is much about today that works best on a social rather than a business level. You can afford to put plans for your future on the back burner and concentrate instead on making the most of unexpected invitations and offers of social treats.

27 THURSDAY
Moon Age Day 23   Moon Sign Scorpio

am ....

pm..
It seems that industry and hard work should be very much up your street right now, and as Capricorn often does, you have scope to really apply yourself to things that need doing. Bear in mind that not everyone around you will be pulling their weight as much as you are, so be prepared to work that much harder as a result.

28 FRIDAY

Moon Age Day 24   Moon Sign Scorpio

am ....

pm...
This may not be the best period of the month for personal gratification and you need to be ready to deal with a few frustrations under present planetary trends. The emphasis is also on the attention you give to loved ones and the time you set aside especially for them. The more you take others into account, the better your own life should be.

29 SATURDAY

Moon Age Day 25   Moon Sign Sagittarius

am ....

pm...
It's time to show your generosity across the board, and to ensure that it isn't only people you know well who are on the receiving end of your kindness. Today is also an opportunity to strengthen your finances. This is a favourable period for fundraising activities and for also showing the more charitable side of your Earth-sign nature.

30 SUNDAY

Moon Age Day 26   Moon Sign Sagittarius

am ....

pm...
The Moon is now in your solar twelfth house, indicating a tendency to be slightly more susceptible to deception, so there is all the more reason to keep your eyes open. It might not be sensible to try and keep up the level of energy and determination that have typified you this month, but by tomorrow you can get everything back to normal.

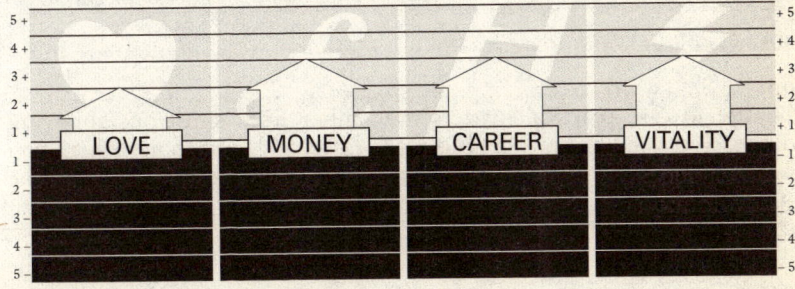

31 MONDAY

Moon Age Day 27   Moon Sign Capricorn

am ....

pm..

Now you can really try out your luck. The Moon is back in your zodiac sign and this is the start of a week during which you can make almost anything happen. Don't allow anyone to change your mind once it is made up, and be willing to go that extra mile in order to get what you want. You can clearly get Lady Luck on your side under present trends.

1 TUESDAY

Moon Age Day 28   Moon Sign Capricorn

am ....

pm..

Right now you have the ability to talk almost anyone into anything, which makes this not only the first day of February but also one of the most potentially successful days of the month. Now is the time to go straight after what you want, without allowing things to get in your way. Might some people even call you ruthless at present?

2 WEDNESDAY

Moon Age Day 29   Moon Sign Aquarius

am ....

pm..

It is clear that friendship is one of the best areas of life at this time and there is much to be said for spending time with those you care for. Pals are usually there for a long time in the Capricorn life, though it is entirely possible for you to form new associations around this time. At work you should be right on the button.

3 THURSDAY

Moon Age Day 0   Moon Sign Aquarius

am ....

pm..

Beware in case practical matters now suffer from small but annoying delays. You need to be willing to work extremely hard to get where you want to go, and to deal with changes in arrangements. Whatever the stumbling blocks, it's simply a question of working your way through them in order to succeed at the moment.

4 FRIDAY
Moon Age Day 1   Moon Sign Aquarius

am ....

pm ....
Things look up again and recent work efforts could now begin to pay quite handsome dividends, even though some of these might seem to be rather late arriving. You can make life more secure with the Sun in your solar second house, and should be capitalising on gains from surprising directions, some of which you might have forgotten.

5 SATURDAY
Moon Age Day 2   Moon Sign Pisces

am ....

pm ....
Does relating to others at a personal level seem to have its downside now? If so, you may decide to spend more time with friends this weekend. By all means do what you can to bolster the confidence of your partner, but remember that you can't live the life of another individual for them, no matter how close you may be to that person.

6 SUNDAY
Moon Age Day 3   Moon Sign Pisces

am ....

pm ....
Aspects of your personal life, and especially romance, are highlighted by present trends. This might be the best time of all to let people know how you feel about them. In some cases this takes genuine courage, but that's what is on offer if you plumb the depths of your own strengths today. The results could be surprising!

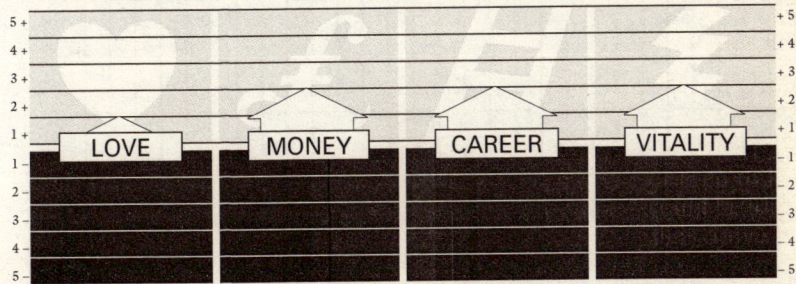

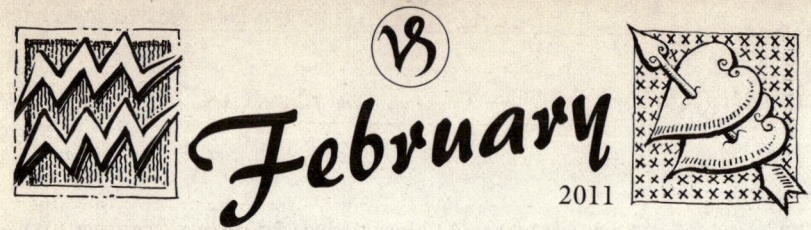

February
2011

YOUR MONTH AT A GLANCE

⊕ = Opportunities are around ⊖ = Be on the defensive ○ = Life is pretty ordinary

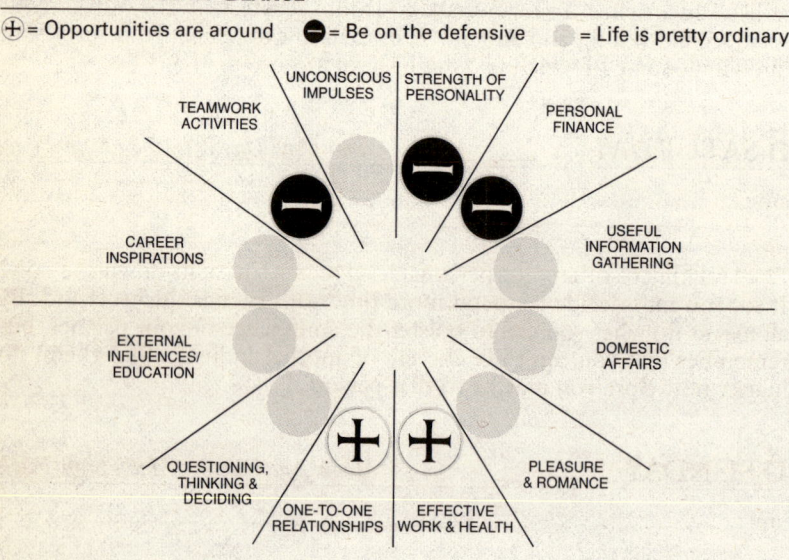

TEAMWORK ACTIVITIES
UNCONSCIOUS IMPULSES
STRENGTH OF PERSONALITY
PERSONAL FINANCE
CAREER INSPIRATIONS
USEFUL INFORMATION GATHERING
EXTERNAL INFLUENCES/ EDUCATION
DOMESTIC AFFAIRS
QUESTIONING, THINKING & DECIDING
ONE-TO-ONE RELATIONSHIPS
EFFECTIVE WORK & HEALTH
PLEASURE & ROMANCE

FEBRUARY HIGHS AND LOWS

Here I show you how the rhythms of the Moon will affect you this month. Like the tide, your energies and abilities will rise and fall with its pattern. When it is above the centre line, go for it, when it is below, you should be resting.

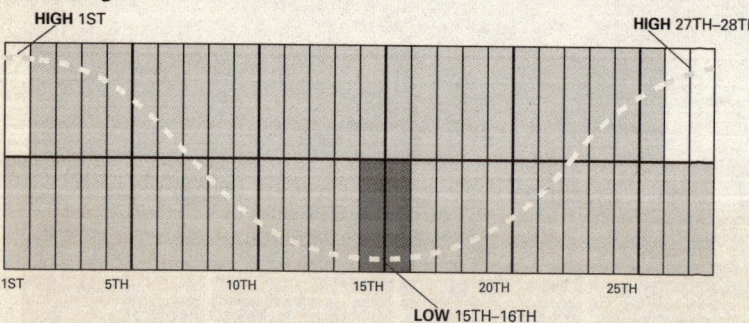

HIGH 1ST

HIGH 27TH–28TH

1ST   5TH   10TH   15TH   20TH   25TH

LOW 15TH–16TH

7 MONDAY
Moon Age Day 4   Moon Sign Aries

am ....

pm..
The time is right to come up with some ideas for making money and for ensuring your overall success during this period. It can be a really positive start to the week for most Capricorn people, particularly if you can obtain support for any proposals you put forward. The spotlight is on attention to detail, and on how you follow through.

8 TUESDAY
Moon Age Day 5   Moon Sign Aries

am ....

pm..
You will no doubt have private goals you wish to realise, and it's worth persuading others to back your schemes too. This might mean talking a good deal more than you sometimes do and explaining the way your mind is working. Giving more attention to your domestic life can also make a great deal of difference around now.

9 WEDNESDAY
Moon Age Day 6   Moon Sign Aries

am ....

pm..
Trends encourage you to gain better control of your finances, which is something you often give a great deal of thought to. It is possible you may decide to be more frugal for a short time, or else do something different with your savings. Either way, even if you aren't exactly obsessed with money, there's no harm in keeping such issues in mind.

10 THURSDAY
Moon Age Day 7   Moon Sign Taurus

am ....

pm..
By all means try to improve cash flow, though there may be other things demanding your attention now. Matters generally can be negotiated, without the delays that sometimes dog you, and the more talkative side of your nature is still to the fore. Be prepared to help friends who are relying heavily on you today.

11 FRIDAY

Moon Age Day 8   Moon Sign Taurus

am ....

pm ....
A strong social influence is evident, thanks to the present position of the Moon in your solar chart. This would be an ideal time to get out there and mix with people, and to show them the genuinely gregarious side of your Capricorn nature. Take full advantage of this tendency to put yourself in the mainstream and soak up the limelight.

12 SATURDAY

Moon Age Day 9   Moon Sign Gemini

am ....

pm ....
Experiencing better and better job security is something that is important to Capricorn, and present trends give you an opportunity to spend time this weekend working out how you can achieve this. In between all the thinking you can still afford to socialise, in some cases with people you didn't know well before.

13 SUNDAY

Moon Age Day 10   Moon Sign Gemini

am ....

pm ....
With Venus in your own zodiac sign around now, you have the ability to show how courteous and compliant you can be. It is also a favourable period to pursue better times as far as your own personal life is concerned. You have what it takes to get on well with people generally, and should be doing all you can to get yourself involved in new social ventures.

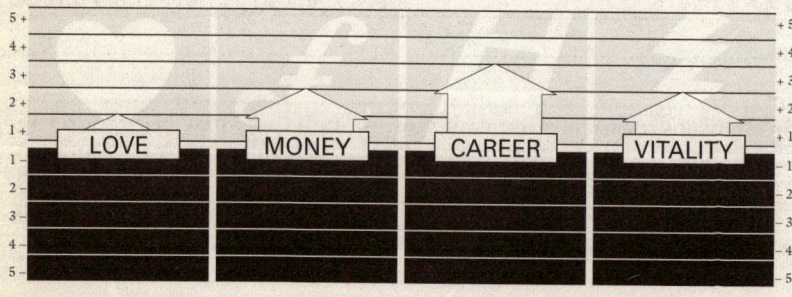

14 MONDAY   *Moon Age Day 11   Moon Sign Gemini*

am ....

pm...
This is the last day before the month's lunar low, which is why it's worth
firming up plans and getting any necessary tasks out of the way as quickly
as you can. Don't be too willing to take on jobs that are difficult and
which will extend into tomorrow. In other words, it would be sensible to
leave your schedule as free as possible.

15 TUESDAY   *Moon Age Day 12   Moon Sign Cancer*

am ....

pm...
Today calls for a lower profile, and you should be quite happy to watch
and wait much more than has been the case for the last few days. By
all means catch up on unfinished business, though you need to do so
steadily. This is certainly not the best part of the month to crowd your
schedule to such an extent that you have no time to think.

16 WEDNESDAY   *Moon Age Day 13   Moon Sign Cancer*

am ....

pm...
The lull is still in operation, though as long as you are not expecting too
much of yourself you can afford to feel fairly contented with the way life
is going. Astrology is all about 'taking the hint', and that is certainly true
today. Be willing to watch what is going on around you, without feeling
that you have to be involved at every stage.

17 THURSDAY   *Moon Age Day 14   Moon Sign Leo*

am ....

pm...
This is a favourable time for business communications and for making an
effort to get right back at the front of things again. Long-term plans can
be clarified and your thinking tends to be quite realistic. Today should
also be good for investments and for giving your mind to the sort of
strategies you may wish to adopt in a few weeks.

18 FRIDAY

Moon Age Day 15   Moon Sign Leo

am...

pm...
Be ready to glean information from discussions with others, and don't be afraid to allow your mind to wander a good deal more than might normally be the case. This doesn't mean you have to stop being a pragmatist at heart, but there are good reasons to let your thoughts enter places you would normally shun. Remember that a change is as good as a rest.

19 SATURDAY

Moon Age Day 16   Moon Sign Virgo

am...

pm...
Using your money wisely is all very well, though you need to avoid being seen as a skinflint. A few pounds laid out wisely can do no end of good for your social and even your personal reputation, and can help you to gain new friends. That's quite appropriate, especially if you also focus on charity and what you can do for others this weekend.

20 SUNDAY

Moon Age Day 17   Moon Sign Virgo

am...

pm...
A hectic phase lies ahead of you and events could well be gaining pace of their own accord. Keeping up with a world that is constantly changing can sometimes seem to be difficult, but this needn't be the case right now. Mercury is in your solar second house, giving you all the assistance you need in order to be original and quick to catch on.

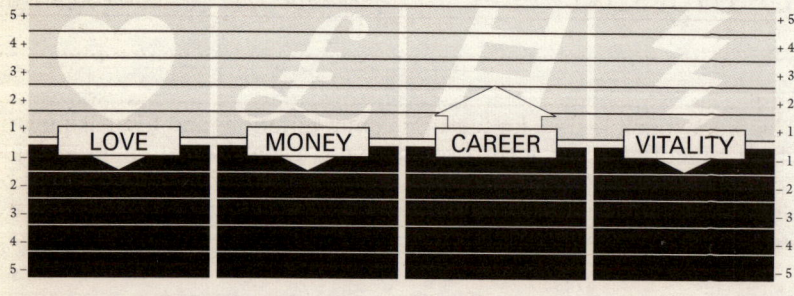

21 MONDAY
Moon Age Day 18   Moon Sign Libra

am...

pm...
You can further your own aims and objectives at this time thanks to your great efficiency. Trends indicate you won't be putting one iota of effort more than is necessary into anything, and this should leave you fresh and willing to take on the next challenge. In other words you can be super-efficient at this time – a Capricorn dream!

22 TUESDAY
Moon Age Day 19   Moon Sign Libra

am...

pm...
All communication issues are well accented now that the Sun is in your solar third house. This assists you to know instinctively what to say to people, and how to express it. Make the most of opportunities to increase your popularity and get others on board with your ideas. There are possible gains to be made when you are in social settings.

23 WEDNESDAY
Moon Age Day 20   Moon Sign Scorpio

am...

pm...
You now have scope to enjoy greater freedoms. It is possible that some restrictions have been lifted, leaving you feeling much better about yourself and about life in general. Getting together with groups or associations would be no bad thing, so why not find a new club to join? Confidence to move forward is there for the taking.

24 THURSDAY
Moon Age Day 21   Moon Sign Scorpio

am...

pm...
Do your best to avoid hasty or impulsive actions today. Mars is now in your solar third house, and it could encourage you to speak out without thinking too much beforehand. You also need to be careful not to inspire mishaps as a result of rushing into things – something you rarely do. In a general sense you can make positive progress today.

25 FRIDAY
Moon Age Day 22   Moon Sign Sagittarius

am ....

pm ....
Today is about how you use your great intuitive insight and your willingness to back your hunches to a great extent. To Capricorn, the way forward generally is by way of looking at the evidence, but this is not necessarily the case to the same extent under present trends. Learn to know that when your intuition calls, you should probably answer it.

26 SATURDAY
Moon Age Day 23   Moon Sign Sagittarius

am ....

pm ....
Your tongue and wit are both sharp – so much so that you might just cut yourself if you are not careful! It's natural to want to utilise your restless energy, even though the Moon is presently in your solar twelfth house, which indicates you might be trying to do more than you should. Today is a time to think, so that you can act tomorrow.

27 SUNDAY
Moon Age Day 24   Moon Sign Capricorn

am ....

pm ....
Today is about finding opportunities to try something new now that the lunar high has arrived. Whatever you take on, you have scope to make a success of it and you can easily impress anyone while you are simply pursuing your own goals. Even if it isn't obvious that you are being watched at this time, you shouldn't rule out this possibility.

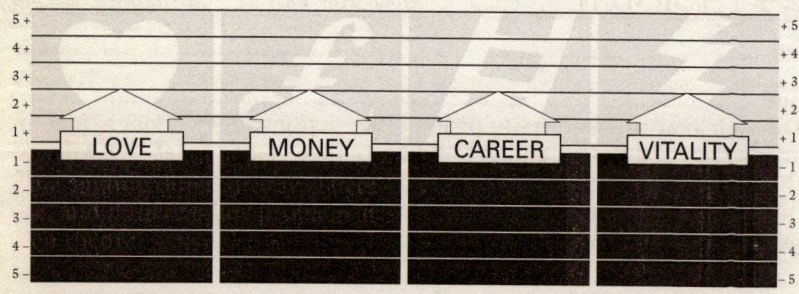

28 MONDAY *Moon Age Day 25   Moon Sign Capricorn*

am ....

pm...
There should be little to stand in your way and everything to play for
in a material sense as the lunar high continues. Pursuing your aims and
ambitions becomes easier and you can tap into a greater degree of luck.
Your approach to the world at large is so confident that you won't be
denied any reasonable request, and the world is your oyster.

1 TUESDAY *Moon Age Day 26   Moon Sign Capricorn*

am ....

pm...
The planetary emphasis is on money. The lunar high is still around at the
start of today and then the Moon moves on into your solar second house.
If you know what you want from life, in most circumstances you should
also have a very good idea how you might get it. Even if it's a question of
hard work – that's fine by you!

2 WEDNESDAY *Moon Age Day 27   Moon Sign Aquarius*

am ....

pm...
Things remain sound and money matters are still well starred, though if
you find you are short of cash at the moment, some careful thought will
be required. Your mind is potentially at its most ingenious right now and
you should be able to come up with some interesting schemes. A day to
seek warmth and support from friends.

3 THURSDAY *Moon Age Day 28   Moon Sign Aquarius*

am ....

pm...
Your love life and all relationship issues prove to be highly rewarding,
at least in a potential sense. It's worth doing what you can to find time
to relax, in the company of people you care about the most. Creativity
counts for a great deal now, so this would be a fine time to make changes
around your home.

4 FRIDAY
Moon Age Day 29   Moon Sign Pisces

am ....

pm ....
A policy of slow and steady progress isn't in the least alien to your nature. As a result, you are able to adjust if you have to go with the flow, and you may not even spend too much time worrying about the fact today. This is the best time of the month for concrete jobs that need your very special touch, and also for some solid planning.

5 SATURDAY
Moon Age Day 0   Moon Sign Pisces

am ....

pm ....
Be prepared to deal with any minor challenges and even some small confrontations that occur at this time. If you have to get involved in any sort of row, it pays to tackle the situation quickly and refuse to bear a grudge, whatever the outcome. There are gains to be made at home, particularly if loved ones want to involve you in their own schemes.

6 SUNDAY
Moon Age Day 1   Moon Sign Pisces

am ....

pm ....
There are signs today that you may need more excitement than home and family can offer, and that means getting out and about as much as possible. Although you might have to commit yourself to specific tasks in a general sense, will this be enough? Trends indicate that what you require most now is a sense of freedom.

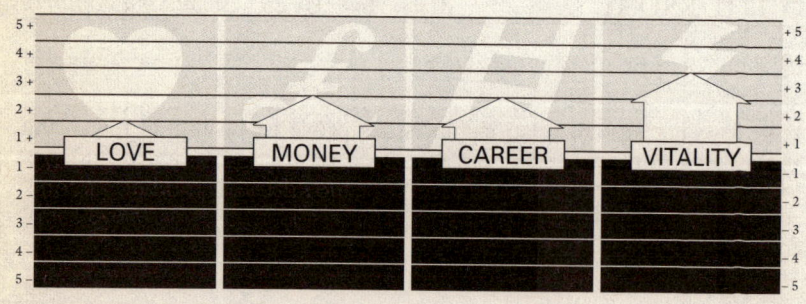

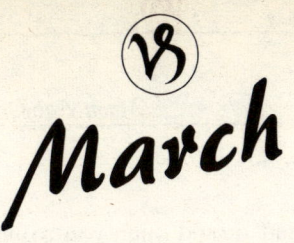

March

2011

YOUR MONTH AT A GLANCE

⊕ = Opportunities are around　⊖ = Be on the defensive　● = Life is pretty ordinary

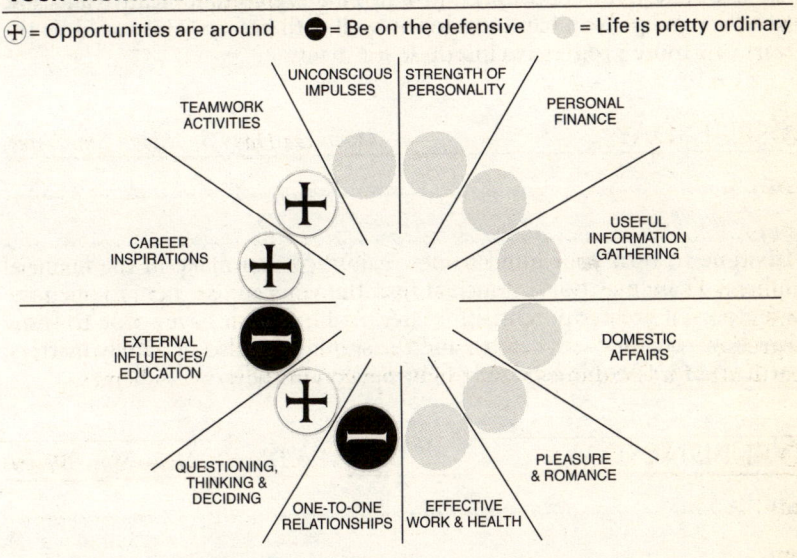

UNCONSCIOUS IMPULSES

STRENGTH OF PERSONALITY

TEAMWORK ACTIVITIES

PERSONAL FINANCE

CAREER INSPIRATIONS

USEFUL INFORMATION GATHERING

EXTERNAL INFLUENCES/ EDUCATION

DOMESTIC AFFAIRS

QUESTIONING, THINKING & DECIDING

PLEASURE & ROMANCE

ONE-TO-ONE RELATIONSHIPS

EFFECTIVE WORK & HEALTH

MARCH HIGHS AND LOWS

Here I show you how the rhythms of the Moon will affect you this month. Like the tide, your energies and abilities will rise and fall with its pattern. When it is above the centre line, go for it, when it is below, you should be resting.

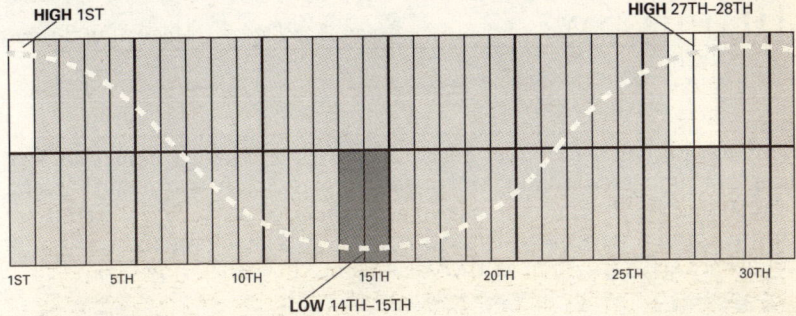

HIGH 1ST

HIGH 27TH–28TH

1ST　5TH　10TH　15TH　20TH　25TH　30TH

LOW 14TH–15TH

7 MONDAY

Moon Age Day 2   Moon Sign Aries

am ....

pm..

Your lightning-quick mind should open you to new thoughts and new possibilities today. Mercury is in a favourable position for you at the moment and it also encourages you to be more communicative and able to talk to people you have not got on well with before. This could be the start of a more progressive interlude for many.

8 TUESDAY

Moon Age Day 3   Moon Sign Aries

am ....

pm..

It's time to turn your mind to new gains you can make in the financial sphere. These may not be much at first, but you can use them to open the way to even greater potential for later. At home you have scope to show just how romantic you can be, and the spotlight is also on family matters, with younger people especially figuring significantly.

9 WEDNESDAY

Moon Age Day 4   Moon Sign Taurus

am ....

pm..

Are you feeling active and alert? If so, this would be an ideal time to turn your mind once again in the direction of some fairly progressive financial incentives. Capricorn is a sign that loves to feather its own nest for later, and you have great potential at the moment for getting most of what you want. Communications of all sorts are still well highlighted.

10 THURSDAY

Moon Age Day 5   Moon Sign Taurus

am ....

pm..

This has potential to be an advantageous time when it comes to love and attachments of all kinds. You can be particularly warm and sincere, and should be showing the fact in all manner of ways. Social trends are positive, and it pays to be aware that the year is changing and the lighter nights are arriving. All in all there is much to be gained now.

11 FRIDAY

Moon Age Day 6   Moon Sign Taurus

am ....

pm ....
You shouldn't expect everything to turn out quite as you had anticipated at work. Remember that life can be complicated, and you might have to delve hard in order to find some of the answers you need. With the Moon in your solar sixth house, you need to be ready to deal with any sudden practical mishaps that occur.

12 SATURDAY

Moon Age Day 7   Moon Sign Gemini

am ....

pm ....
Aided by Venus, you still have scope to make headway on the personal front, and you need to make sure that others recognise and appreciate your current level of charm. You should instinctively know how to strengthen your finances and, all in all, March should turn out well for you when it comes to achieving financial progress.

13 SUNDAY

Moon Age Day 8   Moon Sign Gemini

am ....

pm ....
Trends assist you to be more alert and enthusiastic than usual and to present an attractive picture, especially to members of the opposite sex. It's natural to make efforts to please those around you, and you need to ensure your endeavours aren't lost on colleagues and friends, particularly if you'd like them to do some favours in return!

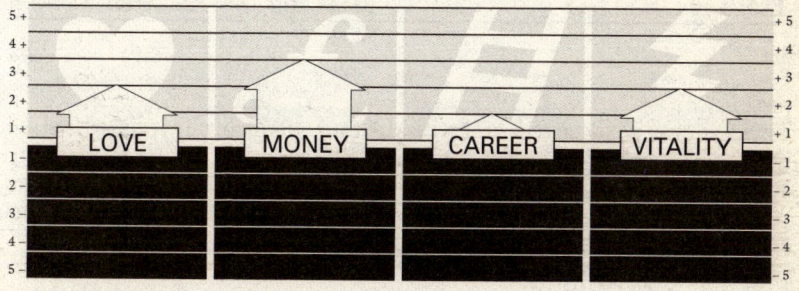

14 MONDAY
Moon Age Day 9   Moon Sign Cancer

am ....

pm...
By all means get as much done on a practical level as you can, though
you shouldn't expect everything to go your way because the lunar low
could well take its toll at some stage across the next couple of days. Risky
business ventures are best avoided, and you would do well to check and
re-check everything before you decide to commit yourself.

15 TUESDAY
Moon Age Day 10   Moon Sign Cancer

am ....

pm...
Keeping a low profile is the key today, since there isn't a great deal to be
gained from putting yourself forward in any big way. On the contrary,
it's a question of watching and waiting, until planetary trends favour you
more. Even by tomorrow you can start to move forward, but for the
moment you might find things a little tedious!

16 WEDNESDAY
Moon Age Day 11   Moon Sign Leo

am ....

pm...
Once again it's time to turn your attention in the direction of money, and
you have what it takes to get much of what you want, though without
having to push yourself unduly hard. Your strength now lies in your ability
to get things to fall into place and to sort out any difficulties that remain
after the lunar low. Seek out some interesting discussions today.

17 THURSDAY
Moon Age Day 12   Moon Sign Leo

am ....

pm...
Travel is now well starred, and with the Sun still firmly in your solar third
house you can make the most of any small changes that are available to
you at this time. The spotlight is on your great need to learn as much as
you can about life, and this is present no matter what your age may be.
Capricorn is truly interested right now.

18 FRIDAY

Moon Age Day 13   Moon Sign Virgo

am ....

pm ....
The planet Mars, which has joined the Sun in your solar third house, supports a restless interlude during which you might be a little highly strung. The position of Mars here certainly isn't all bad. It encourages you to stand up for your rights and also for the rights of those closest to you. Capricorn can be a real fighter at this time.

19 SATURDAY

Moon Age Day 14   Moon Sign Virgo

am ....

pm ....
It's worth getting out and about as much as possible this weekend, since you won't gain too much from staying at home and watching the flowers on the wallpaper. That burning desire within you to know things is growing by the day. Don't be afraid to plumb the depths of all manner of situations, as this will allow you to feed your intellect.

20 SUNDAY

Moon Age Day 15   Moon Sign Libra

am ....

pm ....
This is an ideal time to make important contacts. Even if you aren't at work today, there are still some lucrative meetings to be had. Your best approach is to discuss the germ of ideas with friends, and this could help you to start down the road to a project that can really benefit you later. The spotlight is on your sporting potential.

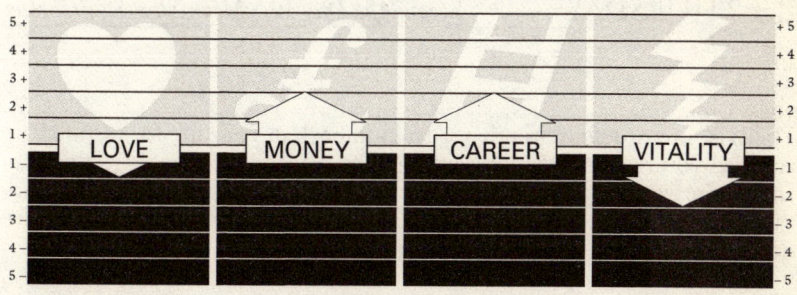

21 MONDAY   *Moon Age Day 16   Moon Sign Libra*

am ....

pm..
You can continue to make the best of financial incentives and should be showing the shrewd and calculating side of your nature at the start of this particular week. You need to build on recent beginnings, and life offers you all the incentives you require in order to do so. Your ability to deal with all money matters counts for a great deal now.

22 TUESDAY   *Moon Age Day 17   Moon Sign Scorpio*

am ....

pm..
The phrase 'never a dull moment' could be applied to your home life this week. You probably won't have much time to sit around in your chair and cogitate if you are determined to keep busy for most of the time. Be ready to discover some happy news regarding a family member, but be aware that this could bring even busier times in the long term!

23 WEDNESDAY   *Moon Age Day 18   Moon Sign Scorpio*

am ....

pm..
Are you prepared to challenge the thinking of others? This could be at home, but is far more likely to be out there in the wider world. Be careful that you don't show what amounts to a lack of tact, particularly if you don't feel quite as tolerant and patient as usual. An ideal time to make contact with a friend from long ago.

24 THURSDAY   *Moon Age Day 19   Moon Sign Sagittarius*

am ....

pm..
There is now a definite tendency to look back in your life for inspiration you feel you need for the present and the future. In some ways this can encourage you to be more pensive and to spend more time sitting and thinking. As a rule the advice would be to push on, but for the moment there is no harm in finding time for some meditation.

25 FRIDAY   *Moon Age Day 20   Moon Sign Sagittarius*

am ....

pm..

This might not be considered the best day for thinking, because your mind isn't too clear on certain issues and you could be going round in circles. It's worth taking the opportunity to seek some impartial advice or at least to explain yourself to other people. The very act of doing so might be enough for you to reach your own conclusions.

26 SATURDAY   *Moon Age Day 21   Moon Sign Sagittarius*

am ....

pm..

The Moon is now in your solar twelfth house, so slowing things down somewhat would be no bad thing. By tomorrow you will be under the influence of the lunar high, but for the moment you can afford to relax more. With every incentive possible coming your way by tomorrow, there is no harm in taking it steady for today.

27 SUNDAY   *Moon Age Day 22   Moon Sign Capricorn*

am ....

pm..

Perhaps it's a case that the more ambitious you are today, the greater will be the number of incentives that come your way. You certainly have what it takes to show the best of your abilities, and you may well be doing more to increase your personal fortune. Getting things to fall into place can be rewarding in itself!

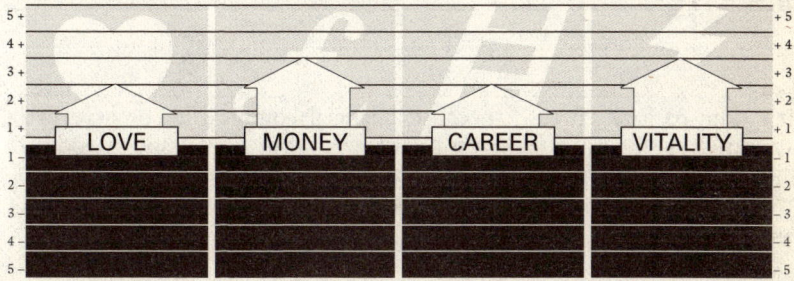

28 MONDAY

Moon Age Day 23   Moon Sign Capricorn

am ....

pm ....

The potential for you to capitalise on good luck is much emphasised today, and you need to start the day as you mean to go on. Even if there are times when the sheer volume of possibilities gets in the way, in the end you have scope to get a great deal done and to achieve your objectives almost totally with a smile on your face.

29 TUESDAY

Moon Age Day 24   Moon Sign Aquarius

am ....

pm ....

There are signs today that domestic issues can bring certain pressures to bear on you. Don't take these too seriously, or at the very least deal with them in a unique and thoughtful way. If certain people come into your mind for no apparent reason today, why not give them a call? Intuition is strong, assisting you to identify where best to put your efforts.

30 WEDNESDAY

Moon Age Day 25   Moon Sign Aquarius

am ....

pm ....

The planets are still favourable for you, and you can afford to be a little more ambitious with regard to certain ideas. What you get out of life at present is directly proportional to the amount of effort you are willing to put in. There are people around who would be only too willing to help you out, but remember that you might need to ask!

31 THURSDAY   ☿

Moon Age Day 26   Moon Sign Pisces

am ....

pm ....

It's time to look to cash, because financial complexities deserve extra attention at this time. Take on board what your family and friends are intimating in a personal sense and put aside some time for loved ones. Even if your life is very busy at present, there is much to be said for leaving periods during which you can make a fuss of your partner.

1 FRIDAY ☿ *Moon Age Day 27   Moon Sign Pisces*

am ....

pm...
It looks as though today has plenty to offer you in terms of making
professional progress. Perhaps new or different responsibilities are
available, and that means rising to the challenges that surround you.
Believe in yourself and it ought to be possible to move mountains – or at
the very least, sizeable hills!

2 SATURDAY ☿ *Moon Age Day 28   Moon Sign Pisces*

am ....

pm...
The Sun is now in your solar fourth house, bringing a month or so during
which you are encouraged to turn towards home and family. It's really
not worth exhausting yourself by worrying about situations that you
cannot alter. Better by far today to address issues over which you can have
some genuine control.

3 SUNDAY ☿ *Moon Age Day 0   Moon Sign Aries*

am ....

pm...
What a great Sunday this would be for entertaining at home! You need to
have the familiar around you, and enjoying convivial company is the name
of the game. Some Capricorn people may be thinking about a health kick
just now, and that's fine, as long as you don't try to do everything in a
minute. Patience works wonders during April.

| LOVE | MONEY | CAREER | VITALITY |

April

2011

Your Month at a Glance

⊕ = Opportunities are around ⊖ = Be on the defensive ◯ = Life is pretty ordinary

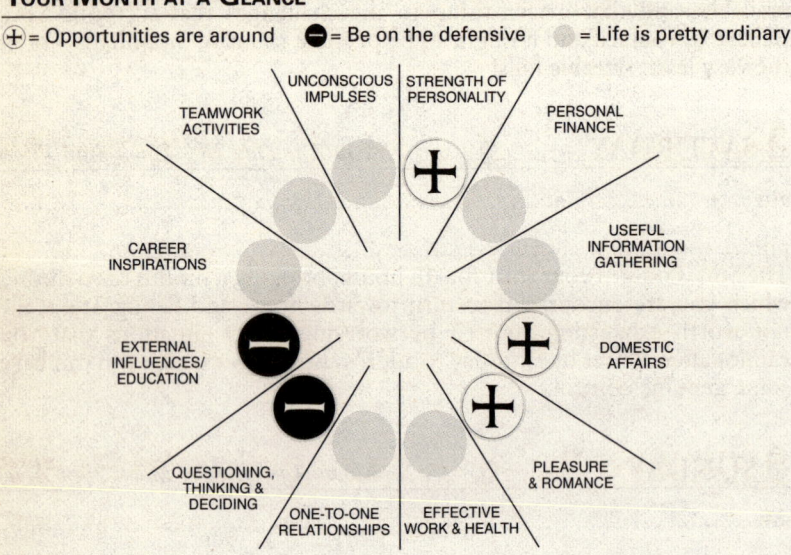

STRENGTH OF PERSONALITY

UNCONSCIOUS IMPULSES

PERSONAL FINANCE

TEAMWORK ACTIVITIES

USEFUL INFORMATION GATHERING

CAREER INSPIRATIONS

DOMESTIC AFFAIRS

EXTERNAL INFLUENCES/ EDUCATION

PLEASURE & ROMANCE

QUESTIONING, THINKING & DECIDING

ONE-TO-ONE RELATIONSHIPS

EFFECTIVE WORK & HEALTH

April Highs and Lows

Here I show you how the rhythms of the Moon will affect you this month. Like the tide, your energies and abilities will rise and fall with its pattern. When it is above the centre line, go for it, when it is below, you should be resting.

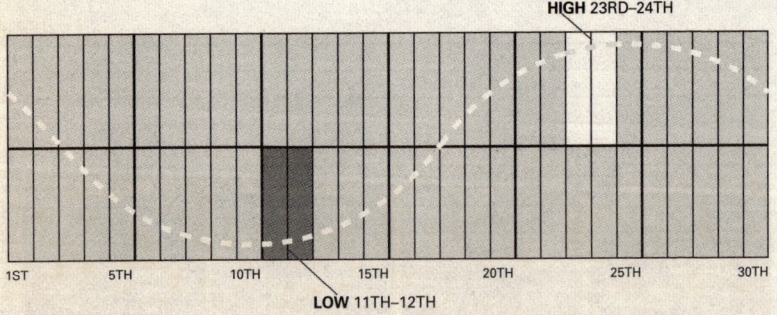

HIGH 23RD–24TH

LOW 11TH–12TH

1ST 5TH 10TH 15TH 20TH 25TH 30TH

4 MONDAY ☿ *Moon Age Day 1 Moon Sign Aries*

am ....

pm...
Today there are pleasant times available if you decide to focus on home and family. There is much to be said for setting aside some time to spend with the people you care about the most. Involving individuals from the past in your activities can make all the difference, particularly those you haven't seen or heard from for ages.

5 TUESDAY ☿ *Moon Age Day 2 Moon Sign Taurus*

am ....

pm...
There should be every reason why you can let go and enjoy the cut and thrust of a generally positive period at the moment. The Moon is in an especially good position for you and brings you better communication skills, as well as one or two surprises that could help you to become better off. Good luck cannot be ruled out at present.

6 WEDNESDAY ☿ *Moon Age Day 3 Moon Sign Taurus*

am ....

pm...
Trends encourage an interest in just about everything today, and it pays to turn over every stone on your way through life, just to see what lies below it. You can choose to focus on whatever takes your fancy, and this would be an ideal opportunity to satisfy your curiosity with regard to the past. Maybe you are looking up ancestors.

7 THURSDAY ☿ *Moon Age Day 4 Moon Sign Taurus*

am ....

pm...
There are people around now who can assist you to get what you want in a career sense, and you should not be too proud to ask for a little help if you need it. It's natural to feel obliged to return the favour, but that is not necessarily why people are putting themselves out on your behalf. Make the most of the affection you can gather today.

73

8 FRIDAY ☿ *Moon Age Day 5 Moon Sign Gemini*

am...

pm...
Your excitability is to the fore today, and you may not be in the best frame of mind for setting the seal on long-term commitments. Is something you have been doing for ages now starting to irritate you somewhat? It's probably worth continuing until you get to the end. Perseverance is, after all, your middle name.

9 SATURDAY ☿ *Moon Age Day 6 Moon Sign Gemini*

am...

pm...
The need for communication is now strong, and short trips that give you something new to focus on can also work wonders. Your curiosity is still to the fore, and there are gains to be made from getting to the heart of certain things. Having to follow pointless and tedious rules may not be your cup of tea at the moment.

10 SUNDAY ☿ *Moon Age Day 7 Moon Sign Gemini*

am...

pm...
By tomorrow you are encouraged to slow things down, so if there is anything that really needs to be done, why not get it out of the way right now? You have what it takes to make this a good social Sunday and you should be on top form when in company. Make sure you demonstrate that you know what you are talking about and that you can also be very funny.

	LOVE	MONEY	CAREER	VITALITY
5 +				+ 5
4 +				+ 4
3 +				+ 3
2 +				+ 2
1 +				+ 1
1				1
2				2
3				3
4				4
5				5

11 MONDAY ☿ *Moon Age Day 8   Moon Sign Cancer*

am ....

pm...
There seems to be little advantage to positive thinking today, except in
so far as it supports you when things are not going the way you want. Be
prepared to deal with minor frustrations, and with anyone in your life
who seems determined to throw a spanner in the works. Patience is the
key to coping with the lunar low.

12 TUESDAY ☿ *Moon Age Day 9   Moon Sign Cancer*

am ....

pm...
Capricorn could be in one of its 'doubting' moods today, and you might
also need to bring your skills into play to sort out some very practical
problems. It could even seem to be one of those days when every key you
hit on the keyboard is the wrong one and when unforced errors are made.
Don't worry, even by this evening you can improve things.

13 WEDNESDAY ☿ *Moon Age Day 10   Moon Sign Leo*

am ....

pm...
It ought to be much easier to tune your desires to those of loved ones
today, and with the lunar low now well and truly out of the way you can
get yourself back onto a positive course again. You can afford to laugh
at some of the things that irritated you yesterday. How could the same
person be so different on two successive days?

14 THURSDAY ☿ *Moon Age Day 11   Moon Sign Leo*

am ....

pm...
Trends now emphasise your sociable and optimistic side. That doesn't
mean you'll like everyone, and there may be some people who you'll
simply have to put up with. On a personal level you have scope to be
romantic and to make someone special love you even more. Uncalled-for
gestures should be much appreciated this evening.

15 FRIDAY ☿ *Moon Age Day 12   Moon Sign Virgo*

am ....

pm ....
Social life offers variety, and there are gains to come from entertaining and encouraging the right sort of people. The spotlight is on looking and feeling at your best today, and this is a trend that will continue across the weekend. In some respects you can gain more from listening than from talking today, but that needn't stop you being gregarious.

16 SATURDAY ☿ *Moon Age Day 13   Moon Sign Virgo*

am ....

pm ....
This might be the right time to bring certain issues to a successful conclusion, rather than trying to carry them on beyond their sell-by date. This could be something associated with making money, or even a personal matter that has run its course. Letting go of a particular memory could be harder – and in some ways even impossible.

17 SUNDAY ☿ *Moon Age Day 14   Moon Sign Libra*

am ....

pm ....
Now you have a chance to achieve a sense of great security and a feeling of peace, courtesy of the Sun, which still occupies your solar fourth house. This can be a steady sort of Sunday but one that still has great interest in specific directions. Don't feel you necessarily have to be sporty at the weekends. Watching instead might be better now.

	LOVE	MONEY	CAREER	VITALITY

18 MONDAY ☿ *Moon Age Day 15   Moon Sign Libra*

am ....

pm..
There are influences around now that assist you to get firmly out there in
the social mainstream. A continued reliance on specific friends or loved is
no bad thing, even though it might irritate you somewhat. Be prepared
for some slight frustrations caused by family members, some of whom
seem to do anything except what is logical.

19 TUESDAY ☿ *Moon Age Day 16   Moon Sign Scorpio*

am ....

pm..
A favourable time for professional achievements and also for convincing
others that you know what you are talking about – even if you don't!
Nature gives you the gift of the gab at the moment and you can use your
natural intelligence to steer your boat towards your chosen destination.
All in all you can make this a positive day.

20 WEDNESDAY ☿ *Moon Age Day 17   Moon Sign Scorpio*

am ....

pm..
Your capacity for great sympathy and strong empathy is highlighted today
– and in greater measure than is often the case. It isn't that you are usually
an unfeeling person, but you do have a tendency to get on with things
and expect other people to do the same. This interlude is all about your
genuine desire to help anyone you can.

21 THURSDAY ☿ *Moon Age Day 18   Moon Sign Sagittarius*

am ....

pm..
Stand by for one of the best days of the month when it comes to creative
matters, and a superb time for getting things looking and feeling right.
False starts are a distinct possibility, but even if you have to start again
from the beginning, you needn't let that bother you at all. The demands
of friends could also bring opportunities for some fun.

22 FRIDAY
☿ *Moon Age Day 19   Moon Sign Sagittarius*

am ....

pm...
Be prepared to take a somewhat quieter approach on the last day before the lunar high. This should be a good opportunity to take stock and work out what to do next. There are some gains to be made in fairly surprising directions later in the day, and a sense that you can make something particularly good happen shortly, which you doubtless can!

23 SATURDAY
☿ *Moon Age Day 20   Moon Sign Capricorn*

am ....

pm...
Most goals can now be achieved through a combination of good sense and prior planning, but there are also gains to be made through simple good luck. Play the lunar high for all it is worth, just as if it was a great big fish on a hook. There isn't much room for doubt, but plenty of incentive to do things you might not have had the confidence to do before.

24 SUNDAY
Moon Age Day 21   Moon Sign Capricorn

am ....

pm...
Your luck is in. You need to do everything you can to capitalise on these positive trends and use them to your best advantage. Keep up your efforts to secure better financial prospects for the future, and take ideas that you had some time ago and make them work in the real world. Things should be lining up for you perfectly on the best day of the month.

LOVE	MONEY	CAREER	VITALITY

25 MONDAY · · · · · · · *Moon Age Day 22 · · Moon Sign Aquarius*

am..

pm..
There are signs that certain everyday issues could well keep you very much on the go today. Do what you can to alleviate any problems that friends are having, and concentrate specifically on the needs and wants of younger family members. By the time the evening arrives you can afford to put your feet up and relax.

26 TUESDAY · · · · · · · *Moon Age Day 23 · · Moon Sign Aquarius*

am..

pm..
The year is moving on, and wide open spaces now become important if you are feeling constrained. This is something that happens to your zodiac sign occasionally, and specifically so at this time of year. The option to get out and about might be more likely at the weekend, but there's nothing wrong with trying to get at least a little time to wander today.

27 WEDNESDAY · · · · · · · *Moon Age Day 24 · · Moon Sign Aquarius*

am..

pm..
This has potential to be a very inspiring sort of day, especially in terms of social matters and specific friendships in particular. You can gain support when you need it the most, and could even find that your heart goes out to certain people who you haven't particularly cared for in the past. You might even be sentimental!

28 THURSDAY · · · · · · · *Moon Age Day 25 · · Moon Sign Pisces*

am..

pm..
Slight reversals are possible now, and even if relationships seem anything but fun and games today, this could well be down to the behaviour of others rather than to your own specific efforts. Are there jobs to be done that you don't care for? Get them out of the way early in the day, leaving time for personal fun.

29 FRIDAY

Moon Age Day 26   Moon Sign Pisces

am ....

pm ....
At the level of your basic personality you should be able to make things happen now. Entertaining and magnetic, you have what it takes to get the whole world to take notice of you. This is a state of affairs that you can keep going for the whole day. An ideal period for getting out of the house and into the wide world beyond your door.

30 SATURDAY

Moon Age Day 27   Moon Sign Aries

am ....

pm ....
This may not be the most rewarding day as far as personal relationships are concerned, but you should be able to make a good impression when it counts. Sticking to friends would appear to be the best course of action now because you want to keep it light and easy. Most of all you would be wise to stay away from family rows of any sort.

1 SUNDAY

Moon Age Day 28   Moon Sign Aries

am ....

pm ....
You can turn this into a generally enjoyable Sunday, even if you find yourself let down by someone you know well. Rather than reacting too forcefully, if you are willing to shrug things off you can show your true mettle and please a number of people. Capricorn should also be showing just how brave it can be at this time.

	LOVE	MONEY	CAREER	VITALITY

May

2011

YOUR MONTH AT A GLANCE

+ = Opportunities are around   **−** = Be on the defensive   ● = Life is pretty ordinary

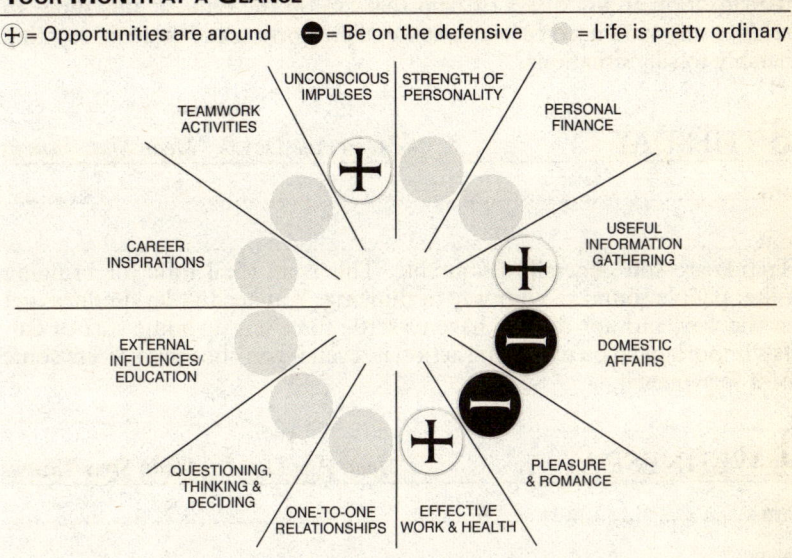

UNCONSCIOUS IMPULSES

STRENGTH OF PERSONALITY

TEAMWORK ACTIVITIES

PERSONAL FINANCE

USEFUL INFORMATION GATHERING

CAREER INSPIRATIONS

DOMESTIC AFFAIRS

EXTERNAL INFLUENCES/ EDUCATION

PLEASURE & ROMANCE

QUESTIONING, THINKING & DECIDING

ONE-TO-ONE RELATIONSHIPS

EFFECTIVE WORK & HEALTH

MAY HIGHS AND LOWS

Here I show you how the rhythms of the Moon will affect you this month. Like the tide, your energies and abilities will rise and fall with its pattern. When it is above the centre line, go for it, when it is below, you should be resting.

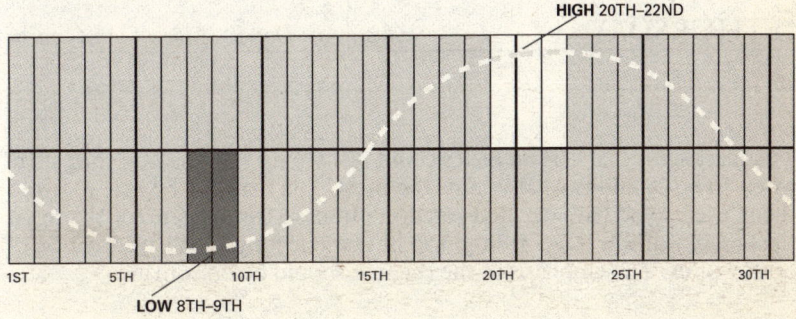

HIGH 20TH–22ND

1ST   5TH   10TH   15TH   20TH   25TH   30TH

LOW 8TH–9TH

2 MONDAY
Moon Age Day 29   Moon Sign Aries

am ....

pm ....
You may have little time for life's pleasures today as obligations get in the way. If you are planning to be a very busy Capricorn, you could do worse than to look at any offers of help that are on the table at this time. In relationships you need to keep a sense of proportion and to avoid reacting harshly to silly situations.

3 TUESDAY
Moon Age Day 0   Moon Sign Taurus

am ....

pm ....
Trends are still generally favourable. This is an ideal time for bringing other people round to your way of thinking. You needn't let tiredness get in the way, and nor do you have to settle for a stay-at-home sort of day. It's important to be where the action is, even if you choose to create some of it for yourself.

4 WEDNESDAY
Moon Age Day 1   Moon Sign Taurus

am ....

pm ....
Mars comes to the fore in your chart, emphasising the very competitive side to your nature, and dissuading you from giving in to anyone. As long as you don't allow this to lead to arguments, all should be well. Woe betide anyone who gets in your way in sporting encounters or over issues that really matter at work.

5 THURSDAY
Moon Age Day 2   Moon Sign Gemini

am ....

pm ....
There are signs that certain issues could be coming to a head on this, a day when to be careful is what counts the most. You may not be able to avoid them, even if you have decided you don't want to concentrate too much on the practical at this stage. It ought to be possible for you to have the best of both worlds. The emphasis in the evening should be on romance.

6 FRIDAY
Moon Age Day 3   Moon Sign Gemini

am ....

pm..
An element of tetchiness is indicated for Capricorn now, and patience may be difficult to find. Be willing to bite your tongue on occasions. Causing a fuss that will reverberate across the days to come is probably not your best course of action. If not everyone will do what you want, this simply means that they have opinions of their own.

7 SATURDAY
Moon Age Day 4   Moon Sign Gemini

am ....

pm..
Out in the social mainstream is where the fun is now. What matters the most is the fact that you can make a good impression on the world at large. This ought to be especially true at work, where you are in a position to influence the decisions of people far from your own personal responsibilities. If you don't work today, go shopping!

8 SUNDAY
Moon Age Day 5   Moon Sign Cancer

am ....

pm..
The onset of the lunar low might persuade you to slow life down somewhat. Never mind, there should be plenty to think about and no lack of people around who can enliven things for you. Keep a sense of proportion over changes that are being suggested by others. If there is something you particularly want today, why not try asking?

	LOVE	MONEY	CAREER	VITALITY

9 MONDAY
Moon Age Day 6   Moon Sign Cancer

am ....

pm...
What a great time this is to be in love and to chase romance wherever you can, despite the continuing lunar low. The Sun is presently in your solar fifth house, a positive position for all personal attachments and also good for consolidating plans. Taking the odd chance today could help you to ultimate success, sometimes beyond your wildest expectations.

10 TUESDAY
Moon Age Day 7   Moon Sign Leo

am ....

pm...
Nostalgic issues come to the fore right now, and you may well decide to spend some time today looking at the past, as well as concentrating on what is happening in the here and now. You can afford to give less time to matters of personal security, particularly if you are feeling fairly secure with your lot in life in a general sense.

11 WEDNESDAY
Moon Age Day 8   Moon Sign Leo

am ....

pm...
Why go out too much when you can entertain at home? This is something that might well appeal to you at this particular point in time. Rather than you going to people, be ready for people to come to you, some of them without any sort of invitation. Getting to grips with a significant issue at work means less problems further down the line.

12 THURSDAY
Moon Age Day 9   Moon Sign Virgo

am ....

pm...
It pays to consider taking a break and a vacation around now if it is at all possible to do so. You deserve a rest and a bit of genuine relaxation, which will probably be difficult to find during your normal daily routines. The more you can get away from business or vocational matters, the greater is the chance that you can genuinely ring the changes.

13 FRIDAY
Moon Age Day 10   Moon Sign Virgo

am ....

pm ....
This is a good time to be presenting things in the best possible light, and this process should enable you to persuade yourself, as well as others, that you know what you are doing. There are elements of doubt around but you can quell these by using a mixture of aptitude and common sense. Look out for problems with mechanical things.

14 SATURDAY
Moon Age Day 11   Moon Sign Libra

am ....

pm ....
Trends encourage you to think about a little expansion in terms of your home surroundings. More space is always useful, and although you may not be able to move house in order to get what you need, a little reorganisation might do the trick. It's time to get to grips with domestic issues that have actually been on your mind for quite some time now.

15 SUNDAY
Moon Age Day 12   Moon Sign Libra

am ....

pm ....
It could be that you want to have your cake and eat it at this time, something that very few of us can manage to do. However, Capricorn is slightly different because you are such a good organiser. Take this together with your present ability to get others to do your will, and almost anything should prove to be possible.

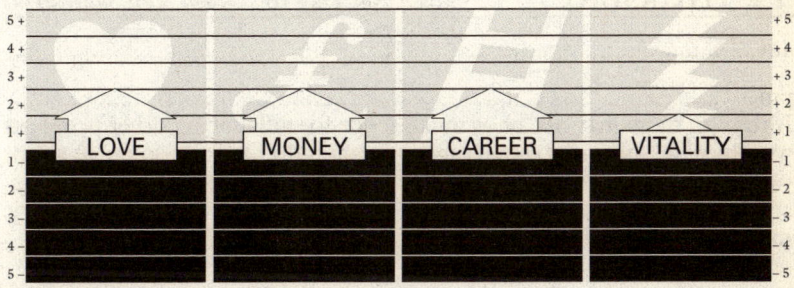

16 MONDAY
Moon Age Day 13   Moon Sign Scorpio

am ....

pm...
The indications are that you should be more content and generally happier with group-based matters today. There are many times when Capricorn prefers to go it alone. After all, you can't guarantee that others will do things properly! At the moment this is less important because you can influence the way those around you behave.

17 TUESDAY
Moon Age Day 14   Moon Sign Scorpio

am ....

pm...
Most social affairs should prove to be a breeze under present trends, especially with the help of Mercury, which is presently with the Sun in your solar fifth house. You really do have what it takes to bring out the best in others and to get them to do your bidding under most circumstances. You may even be able to see new romance on the horizon.

18 WEDNESDAY
Moon Age Day 15   Moon Sign Sagittarius

am ....

pm...
A good uplift from your personal and romantic life is now on offer, and you shouldn't spend so much time doing practical things that you fail to take into account the needs of your heart. In particular it's a question of getting others, or one special other, to tell you how wonderful you are. Be aware that a little fishing might be necessary.

19 THURSDAY
Moon Age Day 16   Moon Sign Sagittarius

am ....

pm...
Although there may not be as much scope for influencing other people as was the case only a day or two ago, you shouldn't worry too much about this because you should be back into that Capricorn way of doing things. If you are willing to do most of the organising, you needn't be too reliant on anyone. Your practical skills are particularly well honed now.

20 FRIDAY   *Moon Age Day 17   Moon Sign Capricorn*

am ....

pm...

The Moon is back in Capricorn, bringing the lunar high and probably the most progressive period of May so far. Almost anything that captures your imagination – which will be a great deal – can now be used to your best advantage. Starting the day early and getting on with things gives you the best chance of achieving immediate success.

21 SATURDAY   *Moon Age Day 18   Moon Sign Capricorn*

am ....

pm..;...

The lunar high continues into the weekend, so it may have a strong bearing on your domestic and social life. With less incentive to work hard today you may decide to turn your attention to what you can do at home. At the same time there is a great urge for change and diversity, and there's nothing wrong with chasing it this weekend.

22 SUNDAY   *Moon Age Day 19   Moon Sign Capricorn*

am ....

pm...

Matters of the heart get a great boost, as the lunar high and the position of Venus combine to assist you to be more attractive and approachable than ever. What really counts today is your willingness to show your sense of humour, and that is certainly likely to appeal to people. You might have admirers you never expected!

LOVE	MONEY	CAREER	VITALITY

23 MONDAY
Moon Age Day 20   Moon Sign Aquarius

am ....

pm...
Even if you feel as though there is a great need to hold onto your finances at the moment, you ought to ask yourself whether this is actually the case. You are usually very much in charge of your life in this sense, and you needn't relax your grip under present trends. Be ready to address any slight worries regarding family members.

24 TUESDAY
Moon Age Day 21   Moon Sign Aquarius

am ....

pm...
Professionally speaking you can now make significant progress. Making others notice that you are around is the first major thing you should strive for. Once you have convinced them to pay attention, it's time to show them just how many good ideas you have. Social issues can be given a boost if you decide to join new clubs or groups.

25 WEDNESDAY
Moon Age Day 22   Moon Sign Pisces

am ....

pm...
Does your romantic and social life now seem to be in a state of flux? Remember that out of confusion can often come something bigger and better. It may seem at times during the middle of this week that people are not really listening to what you have to say. Nothing could be further from the truth, as you should soon have a chance to discover.

26 THURSDAY
Moon Age Day 23   Moon Sign Pisces

am ....

pm...
The Moon is in your solar third house. This assists you to keep busy and on the go, and together with Mercury it also encourages you to speak out and have your say much more than usual. Not that this is a bad thing, because it gives you scope to make everyone listen. All your words seem shot through with genuine wisdom right now.

27 FRIDAY   *Moon Age Day 24   Moon Sign Pisces*

am ....

pm...
Venus has now moved on into your solar fifth house, which enhances
spontaneity and increases your appeal to people who either didn't like
you before or who didn't really notice that you were around. Confidence
is a real hallmark of your nature under present trends, and you should be
ready to show everyone how things are done.

28 SATURDAY   *Moon Age Day 25   Moon Sign Aries*

am ....

pm...
All your efforts in the competitive world can now be utilised in a positive
and successful way. You have a knowing knack of getting things right first
time. This is something that you should be keen to demonstrate to those
around you in order to gain support. This would also be an ideal day to
seek change. A shopping spree might work wonders!

29 SUNDAY   *Moon Age Day 26   Moon Sign Aries*

am ....

pm...
You need to ask yourself whether you are placing unrealistic expectations
upon yourself today. Although you can do almost anything, there are
tasks that will stump even resourceful Capricorn. Be willing to call in an
expert, if only to confirm what you already suspected. Conforming to
romantic expectations might be difficult for the moment.

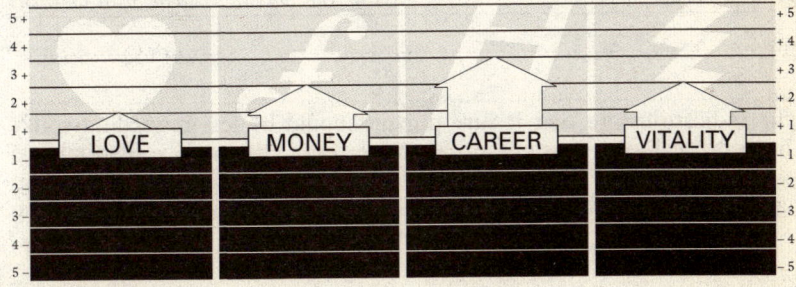

30 MONDAY
Moon Age Day 27   Moon Sign Taurus

am..

pm..
Avoid allowing ambitious ideas to dominate your personality. There is a time and a place for showing how positive you can be, but also moments when the undoubted sensitivity of your sign should predominate. Trends suggest that domestic matters could prove to be more high-spirited than ever at this stage of the week.

31 TUESDAY
Moon Age Day 28   Moon Sign Taurus

am..

pm..
If you feel you are in need of affection today, don't be afraid to go out and find it. It could seem as though people generally are being rather distant and unwilling to offer the support you need. Bear in mind that you might be creating distance between yourself and the individuals who genuinely do care about you.

1 WEDNESDAY
Moon Age Day 29   Moon Sign Gemini

am..

pm..
It is possible that you will find yourself in a rather taxing role as a result of career demands, particularly at this stage of the week. Even if there are people around who would be more than willing to offer you some timely advice, this assumes that you are willing to listen. Capricorn can be more than a little stubborn under present influences.

2 THURSDAY
Moon Age Day 0   Moon Sign Gemini

am..

pm..
The indications are that leisure pursuits could be less rewarding today than practical jobs. Given your current level of efficiency, you should be in a better position to respond to this trend than many other people. You have scope to make a good day better by slowing down the pace in the evening and taking notice of loved ones.

3 FRIDAY
Moon Age Day 1   Moon Sign Gemini

am ....

pm ....
A potentially lucrative financial period is available to you now. There is an opportunity to make more forward progress and it should be easier to get on with those around you than it has been recently. A boost to practical matters could so easily come from family members or friends who have especially good ideas.

4 SATURDAY
Moon Age Day 2   Moon Sign Cancer

am ....

pm ....
Does it suddenly appear that everyone is getting on better in life than you are? Bear in mind that the lunar low has arrived. Pitching yourself against specific tasks is probably not to be recommended right now, and it would be better to find something quiet to do, or else to spend your time looking ahead and planning your next move.

5 SUNDAY
Moon Age Day 3   Moon Sign Cancer

am ....

pm ....
Patience might be difficult to find at present when it comes to making compromises. In most circumstances this is fine. If you know what you want, you can make progress without making life difficult for others. The lunar low does little for your energy levels, and you could be registering this fact in most areas of your life.

LOVE	MONEY	CAREER	VITALITY

June
2011

Your Month at a Glance

$+$ = Opportunities are around $-$ = Be on the defensive = Life is pretty ordinary

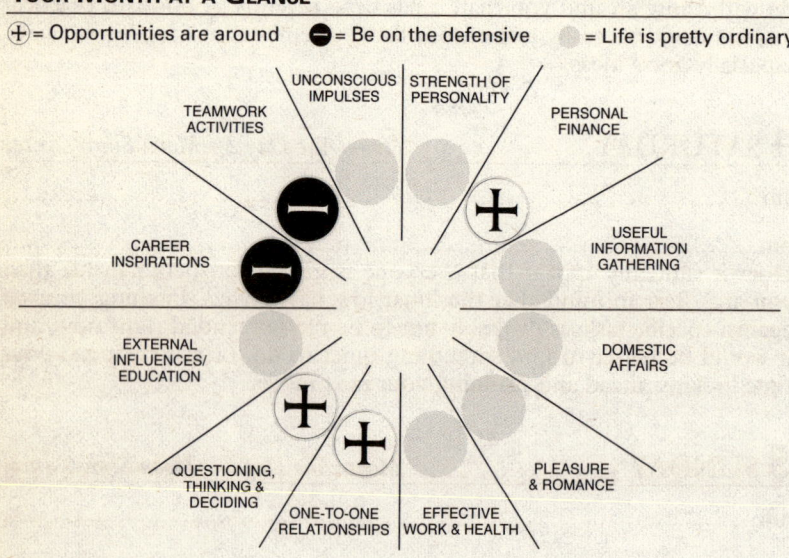

UNCONSCIOUS IMPULSES

STRENGTH OF PERSONALITY

TEAMWORK ACTIVITIES

PERSONAL FINANCE

CAREER INSPIRATIONS

USEFUL INFORMATION GATHERING

EXTERNAL INFLUENCES/ EDUCATION

DOMESTIC AFFAIRS

QUESTIONING, THINKING & DECIDING

PLEASURE & ROMANCE

ONE-TO-ONE RELATIONSHIPS

EFFECTIVE WORK & HEALTH

June Highs and Lows

Here I show you how the rhythms of the Moon will affect you this month.
Like the tide, your energies and abilities will rise and fall with its pattern.
When it is above the centre line, go for it, when it is below, you should
be resting.

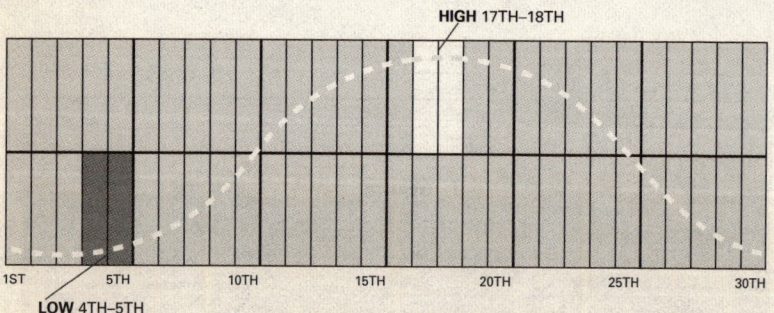

HIGH 17TH–18TH

1ST   5TH   10TH   15TH   20TH   25TH   30TH

LOW 4TH–5TH

6 MONDAY
Moon Age Day 4   Moon Sign Leo

am ....

pm...
Right now you might decide it's best to leave something behind because it will be difficult to keep up with everything and still do a good job of it all. There are ways and means by which you can shelve a few jobs, but one thing is certain, you need to be single-minded if you really want to achieve some specifically important objectives.

7 TUESDAY
Moon Age Day 5   Moon Sign Leo

am ....

pm...
Are you ready for some love and romance? The planets suggest that you are, and this trend will continue for most of this week. The present position of Venus is especially important and it offers you the chance to knock someone off their feet. In the financial sphere this would be an ideal time to try to increase your earnings.

8 WEDNESDAY
Moon Age Day 6   Moon Sign Virgo

am ....

pm...
You have what it takes to keep your patience threshold at a higher than normal level, and this helps you to put up with things that would certainly have irritated you a few days ago. The month of June is a time to show how easy-going you can be, and how happy you are to go with the flow in social settings and learning activities.

9 THURSDAY
Moon Age Day 7   Moon Sign Virgo

am ....

pm...
Freedom and a sense of independence are important to you at this time. It's natural to want to break free from any series of limitations, but in some cases you need to think things through rather carefully before you do so. Some apparent restrictions are for your own good and offer you more in the way of security than you realise.

10 FRIDAY
Moon Age Day 8   Moon Sign Libra

am ....

pm...
Your sense of self-assurance and determination should enable you to tackle something today that would have seemed like climbing a mountain once upon a time. There is something deeply elemental about your nature at the moment, compelling you to get to the root of things in order to understand the way life really works.

11 SATURDAY
Moon Age Day 9   Moon Sign Libra

am ....

pm...
This has potential to be one of your best periods for personal gain and the weekend brings newer and better opportunities for you to get things going your way. This doesn't necessarily mean you have to be able to get everyone to do your bidding. There is always another way, involving a combination of common sense and intuition.

12 SUNDAY
Moon Age Day 10   Moon Sign Libra

am ....

pm...
Practical jobs should be easy to deal with but you might come slightly unstuck in personal attachments. The best way of avoiding this is to look at matters carefully and be reasonable in your attitude. Even if you can't achieve everything you want at the moment, you may come closer to doing so than you have at any time so far this year.

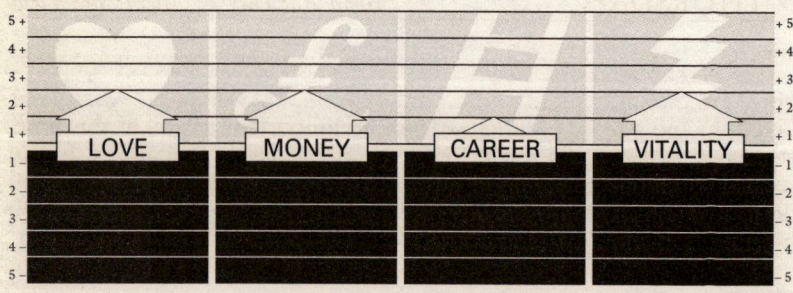

13 MONDAY   *Moon Age Day 11   Moon Sign Scorpio*

am ....

pm...
This is still a good time to make the kind of progress at work that you are seeking, and the Sun in your solar sixth house offers a mixture of practical ability and a deeply intuitive sense of how you should proceed. In affairs of the heart it's important to remain committed, since any hesitancy could lead to some embarrassment.

14 TUESDAY   *Moon Age Day 12   Moon Sign Scorpio*

am ....

pm...
Intense emotions strengthen now under the influence of Mars. The fiery planet is in your solar fourth house, indicating the possibility of one or two disagreements in the home sphere, with the potential for arguments if other people refuse to back down. You know what is right at the moment and won't give much ground yourself.

15 WEDNESDAY   *Moon Age Day 13   Moon Sign Sagittarius*

am ....

pm...
A temporary retreat would be no bad thing as the Moon passes through your solar twelfth house. This doesn't mean you have to retire from anything, but it does discourage you from getting involved in jobs you know are going to take some time. There's no harm in watching and waiting, at least until Friday.

16 THURSDAY   *Moon Age Day 14   Moon Sign Sagittarius*

am ....

pm...
It pays to keep your eye on things, whilst at the same time being patient and waiting for the right time to act. That time isn't today, and so you would be wise to spend a few hours getting yourself prepared. It's good sometimes to retire just a little and listen to what life is trying to tell you. Most of us rarely do it and we suffer as a result.

17 FRIDAY
Moon Age Day 15   Moon Sign Capricorn

am ....

pm...

Today should turn out to be one of the luckiest days of the month, as the Moon returns to Capricorn and opens up all sorts of new doors for you. The impact you can have on life is stronger than ever, and if you impress people with your actions and attitudes, you should also be able to get them to follow your lead. In particular, finances can be improved.

18 SATURDAY
Moon Age Day 16   Moon Sign Capricorn

am ....

pm...

Getting organised is now the name of the game, and you have everything you need in order to achieve your objectives. This is a time of ambition and a period when you can put a full stop to any tasks that have taken ages. Make sure you feature strongly in the hearts and minds of people who are important to you, and don't be afraid to use your influence.

19 SUNDAY
Moon Age Day 17   Moon Sign Aquarius

am ....

pm...

The present position of Venus could help you to overcome work obstacles and allow you to get closer to achieving something than you have been for a few days past. The path to progress should look quite clear, even though you might have to carry people's opinions along with you. Your persuasive powers remain well honed.

	LOVE	MONEY	CAREER	VITALITY

20 MONDAY   *Moon Age Day 18   Moon Sign Aquarius*

am..

pm..
Trends encourage a more communicative frame of mind now, and you
should be doing all you can to persuade the world that you know what
you are talking about. Even small talk can be important when it comes to
getting what you want, and there are gains to be made through conversing
with almost anyone – even at the bus stop!

21 TUESDAY   *Moon Age Day 19   Moon Sign Pisces*

am..

pm..
There are trends around now that assist you to remain very much on
the go and which won't allow you to slow things down very much at all.
That's fine, until you run yourself ragged and then wonder why you are
so fatigued. There should be a few jobs that you can leave to others, but
the problem is that you only really trust yourself.

22 WEDNESDAY   *Moon Age Day 20   Moon Sign Pisces*

am..

pm..
Work and routine matters come under the spotlight while Venus occupies
its present position in your solar chart. You have scope to increase your
popularity with others, to see your objectives clearly, and in an all-round
sense to be quite satisfied with your lot. Romance could come knocking
later in the day – but are you at home to it?

23 THURSDAY   *Moon Age Day 21   Moon Sign Pisces*

am..

pm..
Do you sense a polarisation between what you want to achieve out
there in the wider world and what is being demanding of you at home?
Reconciling these differences is part of what this interlude is all about,
and it will take some thought. There isn't any doubt about your mental
processes, which can be amazing right now.

24 FRIDAY
Moon Age Day 22   Moon Sign Aries

am ....

pm..
Your receptiveness to the ideas of those with whom you come into contact could assist you to make this one of the most co-operative phases of the month. You should do well in groups that have common objectives, and can afford to play the game as a team member much more than usual. Don't be afraid to gather a few admirers on the way.

25 SATURDAY
Moon Age Day 23   Moon Sign Aries

am ....

pm..
If frustrations arise with certain plans, your best approach is simply to remain patient and see things through to their conclusion. There could be occasions today when you know that what you are doing is bound to fail, but you may still feel you are obliged to plough on. In affairs of the heart it's time to show your true sincerity.

26 SUNDAY
Moon Age Day 24   Moon Sign Taurus

am ....

pm..
You can get on quite well with most people on this particular Sunday, and have what it takes to talk even the most potentially awkward individuals round to your way of thinking. There are gains to be made in practical matters, though you need to be prepared to deal with frustrations at home, particularly in terms of the behaviour of relatives.

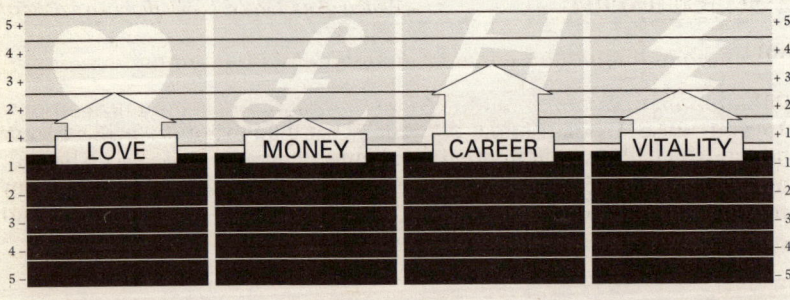

27 MONDAY

Moon Age Day 25   Moon Sign Taurus

am ....

pm...
You should be in the best of company today, especially if you are willing to seek out people you get on well with. The present position of Venus assists you in being as approachable as ever, a fact that isn't lost on either friends or strangers. Stand by to send your popularity off the scale when you are in pleasant settings.

28 TUESDAY

Moon Age Day 26   Moon Sign Taurus

am ....

pm...
Dealings with a wider social circle this week can serve to remind you that your best area of life right now is that of one-to-one pursuits. This is simply because Capricorn, though gregarious on occasions, needs to react to individuals in a positive way. The trend doesn't prevent you from getting on in a practical sense.

29 WEDNESDAY

Moon Age Day 27   Moon Sign Gemini

am ....

pm...
Even if you decide you should focus to a great extent on personal matters, you should still be able to find time to sort out the problems of colleagues and friends alike. This has potential to be a very busy sort of day and not at all an ideal period to sit and reflect on matters. That ability comes later, but for the moment it pays to concentrate.

30 THURSDAY

Moon Age Day 28   Moon Sign Gemini

am ....

pm...
You can make this a positive phase if you capitalise on your popularity rating, which will be emphasised for quite some time. It might be hard to miss this, because so many social situations are beckoning. Keeping your concentration focused on professional matters may not be too easy, and you needn't turn away offers of assistance.

1 FRIDAY
Moon Age Day 0   Moon Sign Cancer

am ....

pm..
A few setbacks are possible as the lunar low arrives today, and it is important not to allow these to depress you. Keep your eye on the ball in any sort of financial transaction, though it would be best not to sign documents without reading the small print. Even if the everyday routines of life are tedious, they shouldn't offer any real problems.

2 SATURDAY
Moon Age Day 1   Moon Sign Cancer

am ....

pm..
There are signs that hearth and home will be your main areas of influence and interest as the weekend comes into view. There is much to be said for leaving some of the professional decision making to others, and concentrating instead on those matters that interest you personally. Reorganising things domestically might be a good option.

3 SUNDAY
Moon Age Day 2   Moon Sign Leo

am ....

pm..
It looks as though pleasure and nostalgia form part of the scenario for an interesting and quite eventful sort of Sunday. Once again it's worth spending at least part of the time doing things that genuinely interest you, and you needn't be held back by people who seem negative at present. Keep your mind focused on issues you know to be important.

	LOVE	MONEY	CAREER	VITALITY
+5				+5
+4				+4
+3				+3
+2				+2
+1				+1

♑ July
2011

YOUR MONTH AT A GLANCE

⊕ = Opportunities are around   ⊖ = Be on the defensive   ⬤ = Life is pretty ordinary

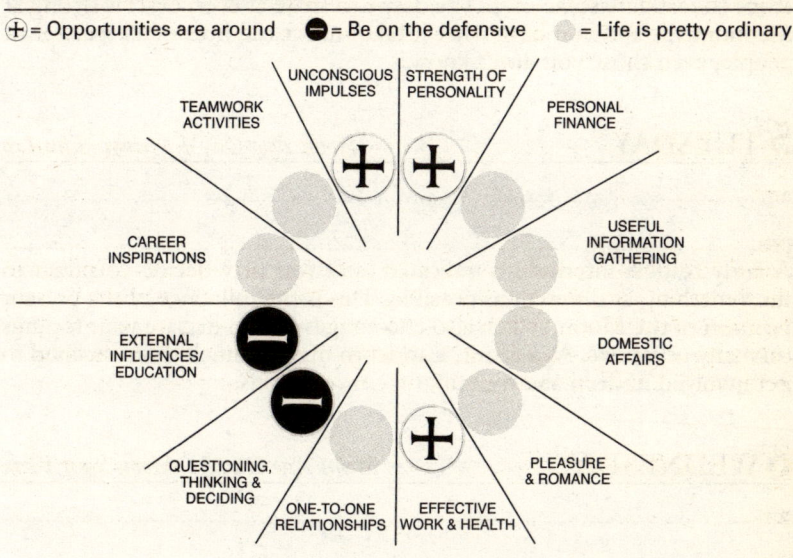

TEAMWORK ACTIVITIES

UNCONSCIOUS IMPULSES

STRENGTH OF PERSONALITY

PERSONAL FINANCE

CAREER INSPIRATIONS

USEFUL INFORMATION GATHERING

EXTERNAL INFLUENCES/ EDUCATION

DOMESTIC AFFAIRS

QUESTIONING, THINKING & DECIDING

ONE-TO-ONE RELATIONSHIPS

EFFECTIVE WORK & HEALTH

PLEASURE & ROMANCE

JULY HIGHS AND LOWS

Here I show you how the rhythms of the Moon will affect you this month. Like the tide, your energies and abilities will rise and fall with its pattern. When it is above the centre line, go for it, when it is below, you should be resting.

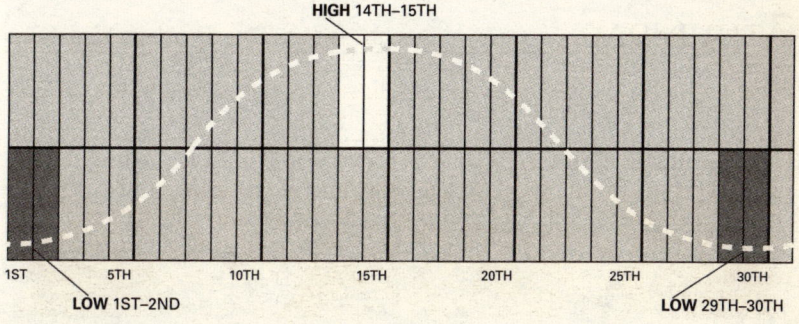

HIGH 14TH–15TH

1ST   5TH   10TH   15TH   20TH   25TH   30TH

LOW 1ST–2ND

LOW 29TH–30TH

4 MONDAY
Moon Age Day 3   Moon Sign Leo

am ....

pm...
Partnerships of all kinds should prove to be rewarding and even good fun today. There is a great deal of co-operation on offer, and you have scope to instigate some of it. The desire to share at every level is strong at the moment, and you have what it takes to lift the lives of all manner of people, even those you don't know.

5 TUESDAY
Moon Age Day 4   Moon Sign Leo

am ....

pm...
A fairly restless interlude is indicated, and you may decide you wish to do something as different as possible. This is the influence of the present position of the Moon, which also encourages you to declare your feelings on many occasions. As a result, Capricorn may be much more inclined to get involved in deep and meaningful conversations.

6 WEDNESDAY
Moon Age Day 5   Moon Sign Virgo

am ....

pm...
Charm can help you to get what you want today, and you can continue to turn heads with your winning ways. Venus is in a favourable position for you at this time and it enlivens your intellect, as well assisting you to be more approachable and more inclined to join in with things. Romance of the soul-stirring kind is a distinct possibility.

7 THURSDAY
Moon Age Day 6   Moon Sign Virgo

am ....

pm...
If opportunities do come your way today you should be willing to take them. This is no time to be hanging around in the background. On the contrary, you need to push forward progressively as much as you can and be willing to trade ideas and schemes with anyone who is willing to listen to you.

8 FRIDAY *Moon Age Day 7   Moon Sign Libra*

am ....

pm...
At work you could well be on a roll and quite able to get involved in anything that seems to interest you, both inside and outside your profession. There ought to be time to do many things, together with more incentive than has been around for ages. Keep a sense of proportion regarding any financial situations that might not be what they seem.

9 SATURDAY *Moon Age Day 8   Moon Sign Libra*

am ....

pm...
Communication remains well marked, and you should be able to impress even usually awkward people with your simple but quite profound view of life. Practical skills are still to the fore, and even if other people are flapping around wondering what to do, you can get things done one after another. A positive time for those who have health issues.

10 SUNDAY *Moon Age Day 9   Moon Sign Scorpio*

am ....

pm...
Events offer the perfect opportunity for you to show your original attitude and approach, and that's the operative point. It's now a question of reacting to, rather than instigating, what is happening. Others probably do have your best interests at heart, even if it appears that this is not the case. Even outside of your usual work you could be toiling away.

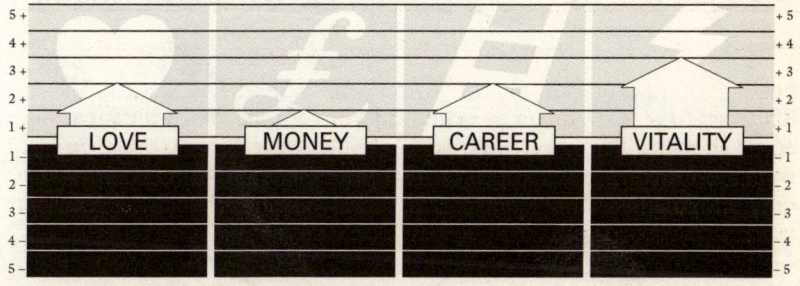

11 MONDAY
Moon Age Day 10   Moon Sign Scorpio

am ....

pm...
You can still carry on making progress, and the arrival of another week should find you keen to get up and go. Of course, if you didn't get much rest across the weekend you might be somewhat fatigued. Bear in mind that this situation won't be helped by the fact that the Moon moves into your solar twelfth house later today.

12 TUESDAY
Moon Age Day 11   Moon Sign Sagittarius

am ....

pm...
With the Moon in its present position you may decide not to take part as much as you have been doing, at least until Thursday. Your best approach is to watch and wait, because the time to act or react is not now. Capricorn people can be extremely patient, and that's important at a time when things are working out well, whether you interfere or not.

13 WEDNESDAY
Moon Age Day 12   Moon Sign Sagittarius

am ....

pm...
Living life from the sidelines can be slightly frustrating in some ways, but is probably your best response under present trends. A more active phase will soon be on offer, and this combines with a real determination to speak your mind. For now there is much to be said for remaining cool, calm and collected.

14 THURSDAY
Moon Age Day 13   Moon Sign Capricorn

am ....

pm...
Stand by to create some new beginnings in your life. With the lunar high come all sorts of new incentives and a desire to get on with things in a big way. You have scope to improve your financial situation, and an ability to use what cash you have much better. Avoid pointless arguments today – you really don't have time for them!

15 FRIDAY
Moon Age Day 14   Moon Sign Capricorn

am ....

pm...

You can afford to be bold right now, but you might also be headstrong and impatient. At least you should be able to get things moving, and you needn't let anyone accuse you of being tardy about anything. Be prepared to change your arrangements today if you feel you have enough on your plate, though in reality you can get masses done.

16 SATURDAY
Moon Age Day 15   Moon Sign Aquarius

am ....

pm...

You can now take advantage of a hopeful interlude when it comes to money, and may be able to take steps towards becoming better off than you expected to be at this time. You might decide on new investments or improved ways to use your cash in the days ahead. This could be a weekend of fun and games, with you instigating many of them.

17 SUNDAY
Moon Age Day 16   Moon Sign Aquarius

am ....

pm...

An impulse to try new things is now indicated, though it's worth remembering that your desire to break the bounds of the normal might be annoying to others. It's hard to move forward right now without causing a little frustration for loved ones or friends. Be prepared to think hard and also discuss what you have planned, in order to make it possible.

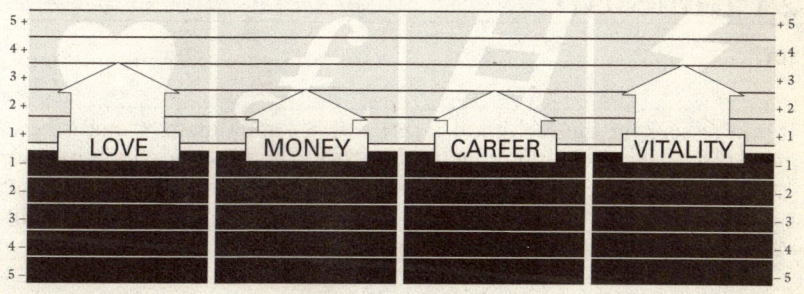

18 MONDAY   *Moon Age Day 17   Moon Sign Aquarius*

am ....

pm...
Trends assist you to create a more hectic time socially, particularly if you make the most of any interesting invitations that are on offer. There may be so much of real interest going on around you that it's difficult to know where to start. As a result, your productivity could suffer. Remember that everyone deserves a break.

19 TUESDAY   *Moon Age Day 18   Moon Sign Pisces*

am ....

pm...
You need to use your mind carefully today when it comes to making choices because there are planets around now that could cause you to stumble more than usual. You are the last person in the world to be taken in by any sort of scam, but this is entirely possible under present trends. Check all details and read every bit of the small print.

20 WEDNESDAY   *Moon Age Day 19   Moon Sign Pisces*

am ....

pm...
Venus now assists you to bring deeply romantic moments into your life. Of course, you can ignore these and carry on entirely with your material life, but it might be hard to turn away from the compliments you are currently able to attract. For some Capricorn people the romantic attention could be arriving from less than expected directions.

21 THURSDAY   *Moon Age Day 20   Moon Sign Aries*

am ....

pm...
If you're seeking the feel-good factor today, family matters might be a good place to start. This is influenced by the position of the Moon in your solar fourth house. This would be an ideal time to make a commitment to new plans within your home and to think very carefully about making some important life change later.

22 FRIDAY

Moon Age Day 21   Moon Sign Aries

am ....

pm ....
Today's trends indicate a change of mind in order to make the most of opportunities that are on offer at work. Although you should be happy in the end, you might not relish changing horses in midstream, and would probably much rather adopt a plan and stick to it. It's time to be flexible, which is not a word that figures prominently in your vocabulary.

23 SATURDAY

Moon Age Day 22   Moon Sign Aries

am ....

pm ....
Renewal and reform are the paths to growth around this time. It's worth making a list of things you know are not going entirely as you would wish in your life as a whole, and then studying it. There may be actions you can take right now to make things better, and more far-reaching possibilities waiting in the wings. It's time to become proactive.

24 SUNDAY

Moon Age Day 23   Moon Sign Taurus

am ....

pm ....
If you get creative in your thinking, the world can be your oyster. It's true that life can be somewhat uncomfortable under a bevy of trends that encourage you to go for constant alterations, but in the end you should be able to make gains during this interlude. It's high summer, so why not get out there and enjoy the sunshine?

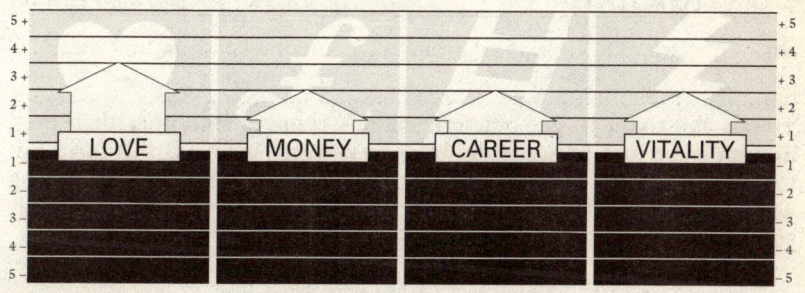

25 MONDAY
Moon Age Day 24   Moon Sign Taurus

am ....

pm ....
It looks as though career developments may need more attention at the start of this working week. Are you now faced with certain choices or even changes? It shouldn't be hard for you to see your way forward at present or to make the sort of decisions that will enable you to feel more secure in the weeks and months to come.

26 TUESDAY
Moon Age Day 25   Moon Sign Gemini

am ....

pm ....
Even if you know what you want from life, you are inclined to be easily influenced today. It is important to stick to directions you have chosen for yourself previously, and not to be diverted by false promises. An ideal time to focus on a special friendship and to ensure it begins to blossom. Your strength now lies in the inner peace you can achieve.

27 WEDNESDAY
Moon Age Day 26   Moon Sign Gemini

am ....

pm ....
A slight hiccup is indicated. Though you can be great company for others, you may not have quite the belief in your own abilities that they have in you. It might be sensible to take a look in their direction. If they trust and respect you so much, why not take a leaf from their books? There is very little to lose and much to gain.

28 THURSDAY
Moon Age Day 27   Moon Sign Gemini

am ....

pm ....
Trends assist you to get practical matters running smoother than ever, though there may be some doubt as to personal issues. If this turns out to be the case, you need to ask yourself whether you are the one making waves. Stand by decisions you made earlier, even if others, especially younger family members, do not agree.

29 FRIDAY
Moon Age Day 28   Moon Sign Cancer

am ....

pm..

Today and tomorrow the lunar low is around. True, Capricorn can often cope better with it than some zodiac signs can, but it still has potential to take the wind out of your sails to a certain extent. Your best approach is to adopt a matter-of-fact attitude and simply enjoy the peace and quiet that a summer day can offer. Relaxation can work wonders.

30 SATURDAY
Moon Age Day 29   Moon Sign Cancer

am ....

pm..

Obstacles of one sort or another could well be a fact of life at the moment, and you may feel there is little you can do to address them. The lunar low isn't around long, but it does support a rather lethargic interlude when you may be less inclined to concentrate. Simply understand what is going on astrologically and you can get things to come right.

31 SUNDAY
Moon Age Day 0   Moon Sign Leo

am ....

pm..

You have scope to improve things rapidly now. Intellectual exchanges are the order of the day, and these offer you the chance to sharpen your mind in a way that hasn't been possible for quite some time. Try to stay away from artificial stimulants of any sort right now. Your brain should be stimulated enough as it is.

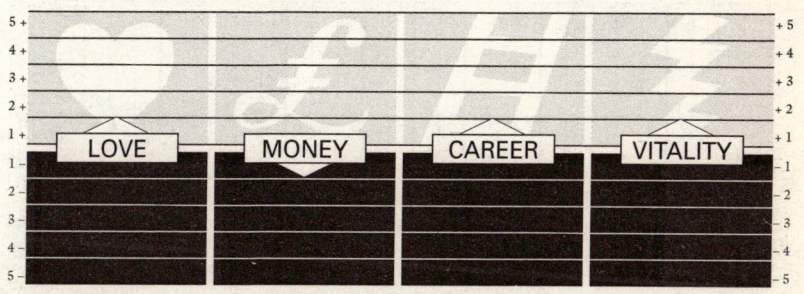

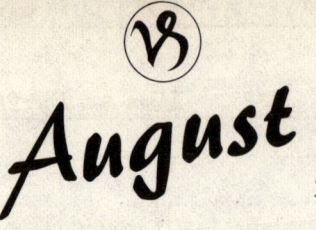

August

2011

YOUR MONTH AT A GLANCE

⊕ = Opportunities are around   ⊖ = Be on the defensive   ● = Life is pretty ordinary

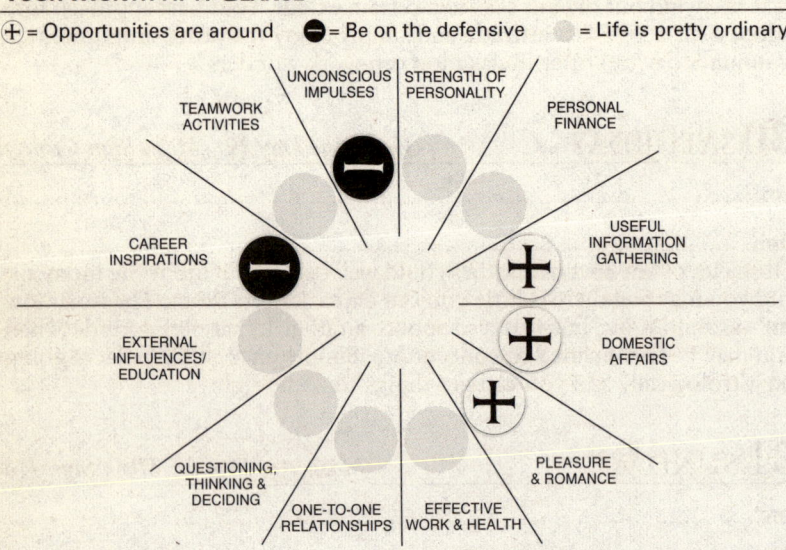

STRENGTH OF PERSONALITY

UNCONSCIOUS IMPULSES

TEAMWORK ACTIVITIES

PERSONAL FINANCE

USEFUL INFORMATION GATHERING

CAREER INSPIRATIONS

DOMESTIC AFFAIRS

EXTERNAL INFLUENCES/ EDUCATION

PLEASURE & ROMANCE

QUESTIONING, THINKING & DECIDING

ONE-TO-ONE RELATIONSHIPS

EFFECTIVE WORK & HEALTH

AUGUST HIGHS AND LOWS

Here I show you how the rhythms of the Moon will affect you this month. Like the tide, your energies and abilities will rise and fall with its pattern. When it is above the centre line, go for it, when it is below, you should be resting.

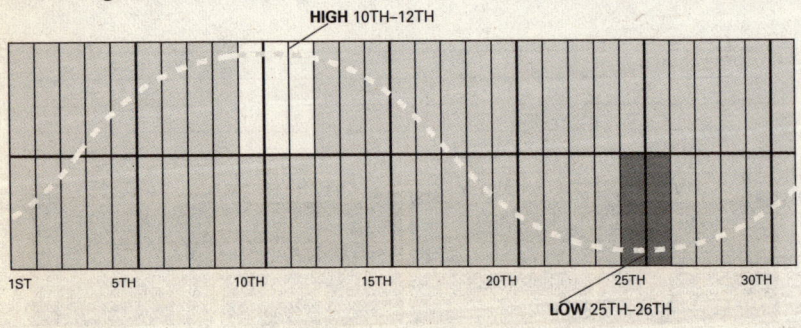

HIGH 10TH–12TH

1ST   5TH   10TH   15TH   20TH   25TH   30TH

LOW 25TH–26TH

1 MONDAY
Moon Age Day 1   Moon Sign Leo

am ....

pm ....
Make the most of a positive start to the month. You can bend career situations your own way and stand a chance of making a good impression on others at the moment. Confidence shouldn't be lacking, though you need to ask yourself whether all those you count as friends are really on your side. Beware of reacting too strongly.

2 TUESDAY
Moon Age Day 2   Moon Sign Virgo

am ....

pm ....
You can't expect life to be all plain sailing, and should be prepared to deal with emotional stresses and pressure tactics on the part of colleagues or acquaintances. As long as you know you are playing a straight bat, you can proceed with impunity. Remember that anything distasteful that you're required to do is best done quickly.

3 WEDNESDAY ☿
Moon Age Day 3   Moon Sign Virgo

am ....

pm ....
A steady approach works best today, particularly if you feel your life is beset with small pressures and issues that just won't work out the way you want. There is absolutely no point in becoming frustrated with the situation. In any case, by tomorrow you ought to be able to get everything on a more even keel.

4 THURSDAY ☿
Moon Age Day 4   Moon Sign Libra

am ....

pm ....
A day to keep your mind working well and to grab with both hands any opportunity to broaden your horizons. This is yet another indication that Capricorn people can afford to be in a holiday frame of mind. If everyday responsibilities make this impossible, you could at least try to get some change and diversity into your life during social hours.

5 FRIDAY
☿ *Moon Age Day 5   Moon Sign Libra*

am ....

pm...
Friday arrives and you should be in a very good position to influence others. This applies particularly at work. Even if a degree of coercion is necessary, as long as you know the end genuinely does justify the means, you should be able to go ahead. Once work is out of the way, getting out of doors is the name of the game.

6 SATURDAY
☿ *Moon Age Day 6   Moon Sign Scorpio*

am ....

pm...
As Saturday dawns the focus remains on your social life. There are trends around at the moment that would make this period ideal for travel, so you may decide that a holiday is on the cards. You needn't allow any of your plans to be altered too much by the attitude and opinions of people who are not really involved in them at all.

7 SUNDAY
☿ *Moon Age Day 7   Moon Sign Scorpio*

am ....

pm...
Trends suggest that what really does matter today is the number and quality of contacts you are willing to make. It is for this reason that you can't really afford to put your feet up too much. Action is the key to success, no matter what sphere of life you are looking at. A strong attachment could be formed as the weekend comes to an end.

LOVE	MONEY	CAREER	VITALITY

8 MONDAY ☿ *Moon Age Day 8   Moon Sign Sagittarius*

am ....

pm...
A slight drop in confidence is indicated today, and you can't expect absolutely everyone to have your best interests at heart. This is the influence of the position of the Moon, but it is a very temporary state of affairs and not something you should react to harshly. By all means let others make some of the decisions, and be prepared to leave them to it!

9 TUESDAY ☿ *Moon Age Day 9   Moon Sign Sagittarius*

am ....

pm...
There could still be some limitations about, though you needn't allow these to hold up your general progress in life. This isn't the best time for dealing with friends, and it might be difficult to see opportunities for real gains. By tomorrow – or maybe even by tonight – you should be able to ensure that any problems disappear like the morning mist.

10 WEDNESDAY ☿ *Moon Age Day 10   Moon Sign Capricorn*

am ....

pm...
Look out for opportunities to increase your good fortune because there are definitely many to be found now that the lunar high has arrived. It pays to adopt a 'can-do' attitude, which tends to be infectious and to rub off on those around you. The general level of luck available is higher, and it's time to feel good about yourself and about life.

11 THURSDAY ☿ *Moon Age Day 11   Moon Sign Capricorn*

am ....

pm...
The lunar high encourages you to believe you can get everything working out for the best. Maybe a little care is necessary, because you are so confident you might consider yourself to be invincible. However, forging ahead with plans is the order of the day, and you should be able to seek out any help that you need.

12 FRIDAY ☿ *Moon Age Day 12   Moon Sign Capricorn*

am...

pm...
The spotlight is now on your finances, which you have the ability to
strengthen under the light of the lunar high. With the Moon in Capricorn
you have everything you need in place to make a real coup, either for now
or the short-term future. You might as well push your luck for all you are
worth today – and expect to succeed!

13 SATURDAY ☿ *Moon Age Day 13   Moon Sign Aquarius*

am...

pm...
It may be time to let something go, in order to take on something new
instead. All of the Earth signs, of which Capricorn is one, are inclined to
hang onto things, and this is not always a sensible strategy. Do what you
can to make life less emotionally complicated, but don't upset anyone by
taking prohibitive action.

14 SUNDAY ☿ *Moon Age Day 14   Moon Sign Aquarius*

am...

pm...
This is an ideal day for new personal encounters, and also for showing
the more competitive side of your nature. Your strength lies in your
determination not to be beaten at anything, and to fight like a tiger if you
feel someone is gaining the upper hand. This may still be the case when
there is really nothing to lose and everything to gain.

LOVE   MONEY   CAREER   VITALITY

15 MONDAY ☿ *Moon Age Day 15   Moon Sign Pisces*

am ....

pm...
You can't expect that your ideas and views will always accord with those of everyone you meet, though at the moment you may feel it necessary to pursue your own agenda whenever possible. As the day wears on a slightly more compliant approach becomes possible, but in the main you know what you want and probably won't tolerate any interference.

16 TUESDAY ☿ *Moon Age Day 16   Moon Sign Pisces*

am ....

pm...
Extra baggage is best eliminated at this time, and speaking of baggage, don't forget that this is the holiday season. Why not pack a case and go somewhere? You should be quite happy with what the summer has offered so far, but there is still scope for excitement if you can see places you haven't visited before.

17 WEDNESDAY ☿ *Moon Age Day 17   Moon Sign Pisces*

am ....

pm...
This would be an excellent time to have a clear-out of your life in a general sense. Capricorn is sometimes inclined to hold onto things but this can mean that you end up leading a cluttered existence. Selling some stuff can make all the difference, however you choose to do it. You can raise some cash and also make life more comfortable.

18 THURSDAY ☿ *Moon Age Day 18   Moon Sign Aries*

am ....

pm...
Your sensitivity is to the fore at the moment, and it is possible that the most chance remark will cause you to become upset. If you realise in advance that this could happen, you should be able to deal with issues in a more logical and less emotional way. Try to remain cool, even if you think you are being criticised.

19 FRIDAY
☿ *Moon Age Day 19 Moon Sign Aries*

am..

pm..
This has potential to be a slightly introverted period. The Moon is in your solar fourth house, encouraging you to look at domestic issues in greater detail and perhaps to shy away from any situations of possible confrontation. A little nostalgia is also indicated, with old faces and places becoming significant.

20 SATURDAY
☿ *Moon Age Day 20 Moon Sign Taurus*

am..

pm..
Opportunities of a financial nature are there for the taking this weekend and you need to be up to speed if you are going to get the very most out of them. Stand by to deal with interruptions today. Even if some of these are joyful interludes, they can still get in the way and prevent you from doing the things you see as being important.

21 SUNDAY
☿ *Moon Age Day 21 Moon Sign Taurus*

am..

pm..
If applied in a cool and a resourceful manner, the Sun in your eighth house can assist you to look sensibly at what you need to leave behind and what you need to keep. This trend certainly has its advantages, and can help you to live a less cluttered and more ordered sort of existence. This is something Capricorn loves.

5 +				+ 5
4 +				+ 4
3 +				+ 3
2 +				+ 2
1 +	LOVE	MONEY	CAREER	VITALITY	+ 1
1 -				- 1
2 -				- 2
3 -				- 3
4 -				- 4
5 -				- 5

22 MONDAY ☿ *Moon Age Day 22   Moon Sign Gemini*

am ....

pm...
Extended travel seems to be a possibility, but even if you can't get away at the moment you need to find some way to bring a little change and diversity into your everyday life. Whether you are taking a physical trip, or even an armchair journey, you can gain a great deal from the change of attitude that comes along.

23 TUESDAY ☿ *Moon Age Day 23   Moon Sign Gemini*

am ....

pm...
Once you have dealt with your necessary schedules, you should have scope to make progress again and can use today to get more or less everything to fall into place. Do you have a job to do that you haven't been looking forward to doing? Bear in mind that once you get going with it, you might get on better than you'd imagined.

24 WEDNESDAY ☿ *Moon Age Day 24   Moon Sign Gemini*

am ....

pm...
Make the most of all opportunities today because the lunar low comes along tomorrow and it supports a slower interlude. It's worth getting things in order and handing out any instructions as soon as you can. You need to remain generally efficient if you are to see clearly how the path ahead of you is going to go.

25 THURSDAY ☿ *Moon Age Day 25   Moon Sign Cancer*

am ....

pm...
There are no quick solutions to everyday matters and concerns under the lunar low, and it's natural to worry about things to a greater extent than has been the case recently. As long as you realise that this is only a very temporary interlude, all should be well. Constant interruptions are one of the things you should be prepared to deal with today.

26 FRIDAY ☿ *Moon Age Day 26 Moon Sign Cancer*

am ....

pm ....
Unaccountable mishaps are a distinct possibility today, especially where mechanical or electrical gadgets are concerned. Rather than rising to the bait that the lunar low is setting, stay cool and calm under all circumstances. It's amazing what can be achieved, if only by adopting your dogged determination – the best hallmark of Capricorn.

27 SATURDAY ☿ *Moon Age Day 27 Moon Sign Leo*

am ....

pm ....
Remember that there is only so much you can manage to control as far as your life as a whole is concerned. Don't try to move mountains, at least not for today, and content yourself with a few of the foothills. If you use your general technique of moving forward one careful step at a time, you have more chance of getting where you want to be.

28 SUNDAY *Moon Age Day 28 Moon Sign Leo*

am ....

pm ....
This can be an ideal time for interesting and ultimately important conversations, and you can certainly afford to be chattier than would normally be the case for Capricorn. There is much to be said for seeking out someone you have known and liked for ages. This might put you in a nostalgic frame of mind, but there's no harm in that.

	LOVE	MONEY	CAREER	VITALITY
5 +					+5
4 +					+4
3 +					+3
2 +					+2
1 +					+1
1 -					-1
2 -					-2
3 -					-3
4 -					-4
5 -					-5

29 MONDAY   *Moon Age Day 0   Moon Sign Virgo*

am ....

pm...
Some care is necessary today. Avoid getting carried away with any schemes that don't have too much chance of working to your advantage. There are gains to be made at present, though these won't all be financial in nature. Relationships are well accented, as are all social and sporting efforts on your part today.

30 TUESDAY   *Moon Age Day 1   Moon Sign Virgo*

am ....

pm...
Some setbacks are now possible in terms of your ego. It's worth being prepared for the fact that not everyone accepts your point of view, or even likes you. This is hard for you to take, unless you are willing to consider whether you actually like the people concerned. Simply walk your own path and do what you know is right.

31 WEDNESDAY   *Moon Age Day 2   Moon Sign Libra*

am ....

pm...
The challenge now seems to be to get yourself in the right place to do those things you feel to be important. Don't worry about possible support because you should be able to gather that as and when you need it. Make sure you meet as many interesting people as possible, and be ready to turn some of them into good and long-lasting friends.

1 THURSDAY   *Moon Age Day 3   Moon Sign Libra*

am ....

pm...
It isn't particularly the start of a new month but rather the astrological aspects it brings that supports a slightly subdued interlude. Try not to be too insular about anything. You should discover that any situation can now be made much better if you are willing to talk about it and to take the appropriate action.

2 FRIDAY
Moon Age Day 4   Moon Sign Scorpio

am ....

pm ....
There's no doubt about it – even if it looks as though the grass is greener on the other side of the fence, this may not be the case at all. Simply plod along and enjoy the gains that those around you are making. There is a definite chance today to recharge flagging batteries and then get yourself up to speed again by tomorrow.

3 SATURDAY
Moon Age Day 5   Moon Sign Scorpio

am ....

pm ....
Social matters begin to offer potential rewards, as do your efforts to get to grips with any relationships that have gone slightly astray of late. Confidence to do the right thing at work shouldn't be lacking, though you could make yourself slightly unpopular with one or two people on the way. This evening would be an ideal time to arrange an event.

4 SUNDAY
Moon Age Day 6   Moon Sign Sagittarius

am ....

pm ....
Capricorn is on form, and the art of good conversation is certainly not dead as far as you are concerned. Spend part of Sunday chatting to just about anyone who will listen, and be prepared to be singled out to speak on behalf of others. You can now ensure that your leadership skills are recognised, even if you didn't think you had any!

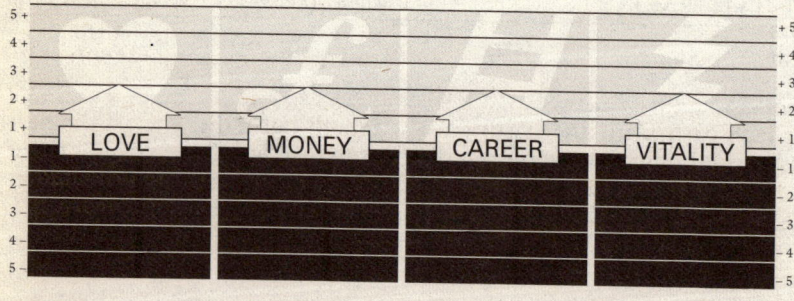

September 2011

YOUR MONTH AT A GLANCE

⊕ = Opportunities are around   ⊖ = Be on the defensive   ▨ = Life is pretty ordinary

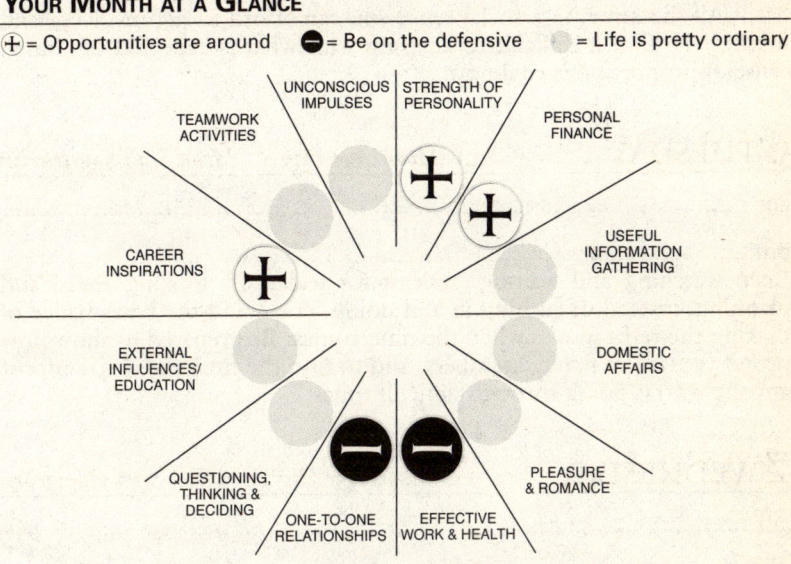

UNCONSCIOUS IMPULSES

STRENGTH OF PERSONALITY

TEAMWORK ACTIVITIES

PERSONAL FINANCE

CAREER INSPIRATIONS

USEFUL INFORMATION GATHERING

EXTERNAL INFLUENCES/ EDUCATION

DOMESTIC AFFAIRS

QUESTIONING, THINKING & DECIDING

ONE-TO-ONE RELATIONSHIPS

EFFECTIVE WORK & HEALTH

PLEASURE & ROMANCE

SEPTEMBER HIGHS AND LOWS

Here I show you how the rhythms of the Moon will affect you this month. Like the tide, your energies and abilities will rise and fall with its pattern. When it is above the centre line, go for it, when it is below, you should be resting.

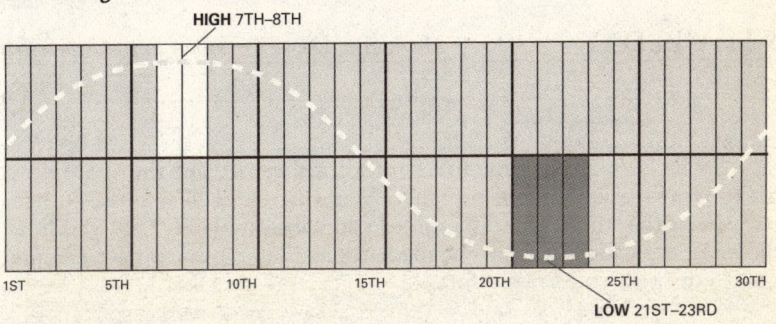

HIGH 7TH–8TH

LOW 21ST–23RD

1ST   5TH   10TH   15TH   20TH   25TH   30TH

5 MONDAY
Moon Age Day 7   Moon Sign Sagittarius

am ....

pm ....
This looks like being a time of fairly quiet retreat. With the Moon in its present position you may decide you don't want to push yourself too hard. All the same, in a social sense you can afford to get involved, and might even find it difficult to keep up with what is expected of you. A sense of proportion is vital now.

6 TUESDAY
Moon Age Day 8   Moon Sign Sagittarius

am ....

pm ....
Keep watching and waiting, at least for today. By looking ahead and planning, instead of rushing in and doing, you stand the best chance of making the right moves when the time comes. Be prepared to show how proud you are of family members, and to find the time today to support anyone who is going through difficult times.

7 WEDNESDAY
Moon Age Day 9   Moon Sign Capricorn

am ....

pm ....
Positive thinking and a healthy imagination combine today to assist you to be potent and potentially successful. The lunar high encourages you to take your natural gifts and use them to the full, even in situations that have worried you in the past. Lady Luck smiles on your efforts, but remember that most of the luck we encounter in life is self-made.

8 THURSDAY
Moon Age Day 10   Moon Sign Capricorn

am ....

pm ....
This can be a go-ahead time in a professional sense, but the spotlight is also on your social life and romance. Stand by to be very busy, perhaps so much so that there are some things you will completely fail to address. There are even some gains to be made today that appear to have nothing at all to do with your own efforts.

9 FRIDAY
Moon Age Day 11   Moon Sign Aquarius

am...

pm...
Trends suggest that you might find yourself running into brief spells when you don't necessarily know what you are supposed to be doing. This shouldn't really be too much of a problem for Capricorn because you are generally good at thinking on your feet. If you are up against any sort of demanding schedule, just cope with things one at a time.

10 SATURDAY
Moon Age Day 12   Moon Sign Aquarius

am...

pm...
You can now be on the receiving end of useful knowledge, even if you don't realise that this is the case. It's important to keep your eyes and ears open today because even the most casual conversation can help you to get in touch with new ideas to fund your life. At best you can be truly inspirational today and can attract the plaudits of colleagues.

11 SUNDAY
Moon Age Day 13   Moon Sign Pisces

am...

pm...
This is a time to be very clear about your current set of plans. For this reason there is much to be said for sitting down and making a list. There is nothing too odd about this for your zodiac sign, because you are generally methodical and like to know what comes next. At the same time you need to be open to opportunities that come out of the blue.

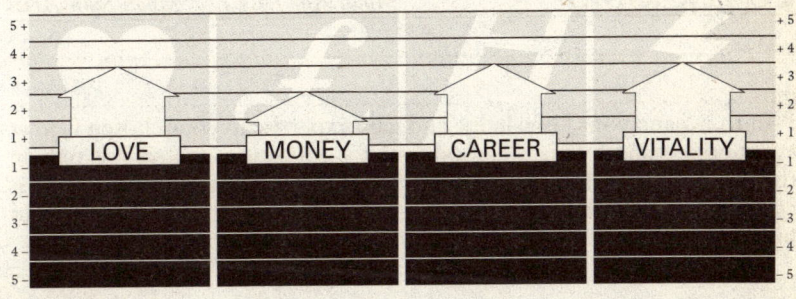

12 MONDAY
Moon Age Day 14   Moon Sign Pisces

am ....

pm..
Travel, communication and other mental as well as social connections can be made today. This could well be the start of a fairly busy week and one during which you should have plenty to think about. Your potential for making money, both now and in the medium-term future, has rarely been better, so it's time to capitalise on your good ideas.

13 TUESDAY
Moon Age Day 15   Moon Sign Pisces

am ....

pm..
It's easy to get involved in arguments, especially under current influences, but less easy to get out of them again. All in all it would be best to stay away from contentious issues, and from anyone who seems irrational and unreasonable. There is too much to do at the moment for you to get yourself involved in pointless departures and rows.

14 WEDNESDAY
Moon Age Day 16   Moon Sign Aries

am ....

pm..
Venus is now in your solar ninth house. This offers a liberating and adventurous period and allows you to sweep away any cobwebs that have been building up across the last few days. Take any opportunity that comes along to do something new and exciting, just as long as it broadens your mind. Love could also be knocking on your door.

15 THURSDAY
Moon Age Day 17   Moon Sign Aries

am ....

pm..
Plan to expand your knowledge and gain expertise in your chosen field at every opportunity. This is a good time for education, even if it is only in the planning stage for the moment. Any sort of course or learning plan is equally valid, just as long as you are sure it is going to contribute to your ultimate success.

16 FRIDAY

Moon Age Day 18   Moon Sign Taurus

am ....

pm...
You are in a position to keep work issues going smoothly today, but can also find sufficient time to pursue some leisure interests. An outing of some sort would be no bad thing today, maybe alongside loved ones or friends. The weekend stands ahead of you. Don't let it pass without doing something fresh.

17 SATURDAY

Moon Age Day 19   Moon Sign Taurus

am ....

pm...
Today marks the start of a period during which you can benefit the most if you allow your true personality to shine through. You needn't let yourself be stifled by others, even if some of them are more gregarious and outgoing than you are. You have a great deal to offer and you can set the world alight if you really wish to do so.

18 SUNDAY

Moon Age Day 20   Moon Sign Taurus

am ....

pm...
Cultural matters are most favoured at this time. If you have managed to organise some sort of excursion for today, let's hope it is to somewhere that feeds your intellect. Strolling along in a kiss-me-quick hat might not be enough for you now, and it pays to make sure you have a chance to learn something as you go.

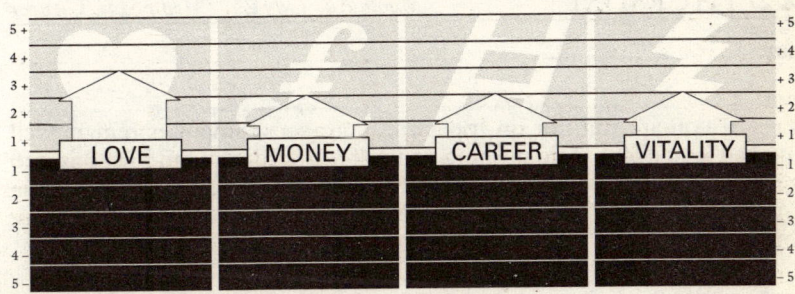

19 MONDAY

Moon Age Day 21   Moon Sign Gemini

am ....

pm ....
Self-control is the key today. There are some potent planetary aspects about, and one or two of them might encourage some fairly untypical behaviour. That's fine at the time, but do you really want to be embarrassed by your own actions further down the line? By all means have your say, but there's nothing wrong with staying just a little conservative.

20 TUESDAY

Moon Age Day 22   Moon Sign Gemini

am ....

pm ....
You have the ability today to flatter other people, which is a good way of getting what you want. Even if you are just being charming, remember that the path to greater progress is open to you, and you could do worse than to play up to people's self-esteem. Capricorn seems to be very shrewd at the moment.

21 WEDNESDAY

Moon Age Day 23   Moon Sign Cancer

am ....

pm ....
This may not be the best day of September. The lunar low is around, supporting a slightly lethargic interlude in which you could feel less capable than you have been so far this month. Why not let other people make some of the decisions? You can adopt an overall supervising role and simply monitor what is going on around you.

22 THURSDAY

Moon Age Day 24   Moon Sign Cancer

am ....

pm ....
Even if you are still not on top form, your social impulses remain well marked, and if you avoid pushing yourself too hard, you can turn this into a reasonably positive and happy day. Everyone needs a little rest from time to time, and Capricorn is no exception. Don't be tempted to interfere with any plans that are at a delicate stage.

23 FRIDAY

Moon Age Day 25   Moon Sign Cancer

am ....

pm...
New perspectives and new ways of thinking should be encouraged, not just for you but for people with whom you work and live. Try to get your colleagues and friends to see old situations in new ways, something you shouldn't have much trouble doing under present trends. It pays to take a more progressive approach than you have in recent months.

24 SATURDAY

Moon Age Day 26   Moon Sign Leo

am ....

pm...
There are good reasons for you to gradually take more of a bird's eye view of life. In other words, it's a question of looking less at the minutiae and more at the overall elements of what is going on around you. This larger perspective can be quite useful, even when it comes to practical matters. You are contemplative but capable.

25 SUNDAY

Moon Age Day 27   Moon Sign Leo

am ....

pm...
This is a day for getting out and about. The Moon is in your solar ninth house, encouraging you forward into little adventures and new pastures. There is great energy and enthusiasm available, something you should share with friends. If you can get everyone in the same frame of mind, why not think of something fresh and vital to do today?

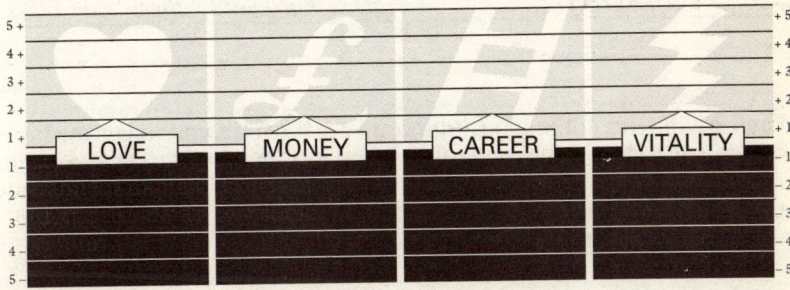

26 MONDAY

Moon Age Day 28   Moon Sign Virgo

am ....

pm...
It's possible that work and practical matters will bring a few frustrations today. You can't expect to make things go the way you would wish all the time, and that won't please you at all. Your best area of focus today would be your social life, which offers far more scope for enjoyment than employment presently can.

27 TUESDAY

Moon Age Day 0   Moon Sign Virgo

am ....

pm...
It pays to ring the changes now. The more variety you can bring into your life, the more opportunity you have to enjoy yourself today. Present trends indicate that you can score significantly more successes than was possible last week. Right from the start, enlist the support of people you know to have similar ideas to your own.

28 WEDNESDAY

Moon Age Day 1   Moon Sign Libra

am ....

pm...
Be prepared to look around, because you could well be making a greater impression on some people than you think. This is especially likely to be the case with those who are your intended romantic targets. Capricorn is not usually showy or noisy, but you can still let people know you are around. Your confidence should be almost palpable today.

29 THURSDAY

Moon Age Day 2   Moon Sign Libra

am ....

pm...
When it comes to communication, you have it within you to get the best from others today. You have a natural tendency at present to fight for the underdog, but before you do, make certain that your support is justified in each case. Look for opportunities to strengthen your finances, through your own actions and the luck that is available.

30 FRIDAY

Moon Age Day 3   Moon Sign Scorpio

am ....

pm...
Trends indicated that most of your truly rewarding moments today are going to come through associations with house and home. Now is the time to find out how fond people are of you and to convince them to help you in tangible ways. Stay away from controversy at work and stick to your own way of doing things.

1 SATURDAY

Moon Age Day 4   Moon Sign Scorpio

am ....

pm...
Although you might be fairly self-centred right now, it is also possible for you to do others a great deal of good. The fact is that you can think up ways to feather everyone's nest, including your own. Sociable and generally kind, there is much to be said for offering a degree of special support to anyone who is desperately in need.

2 SUNDAY

Moon Age Day 5   Moon Sign Sagittarius

am ....

pm...
A day to put your personality to the test and make others realise that you are around. This is no time to be hiding your light under a bushel. The best things come to you this weekend when you are willing to put yourself out there in the limelight. This position is not always comfortable for a Capricorn, but it works and can help you to achieve great happiness.

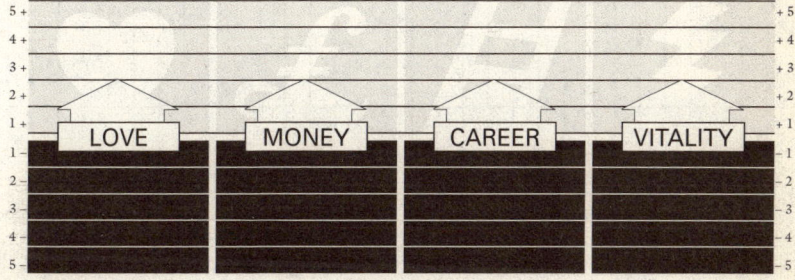

♑ October
2011

YOUR MONTH AT A GLANCE

⊕ = Opportunities are around ⊖ = Be on the defensive ⬤ = Life is pretty ordinary

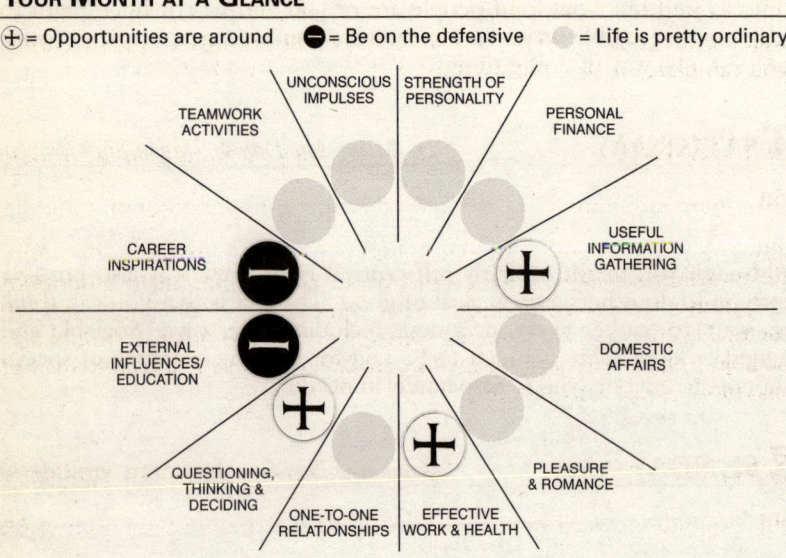

UNCONSCIOUS IMPULSES

STRENGTH OF PERSONALITY

TEAMWORK ACTIVITIES

PERSONAL FINANCE

CAREER INSPIRATIONS

USEFUL INFORMATION GATHERING

EXTERNAL INFLUENCES/ EDUCATION

DOMESTIC AFFAIRS

QUESTIONING, THINKING & DECIDING

PLEASURE & ROMANCE

ONE-TO-ONE RELATIONSHIPS

EFFECTIVE WORK & HEALTH

OCTOBER HIGHS AND LOWS

Here I show you how the rhythms of the Moon will affect you this month. Like the tide, your energies and abilities will rise and fall with its pattern. When it is above the centre line, go for it, when it is below, you should be resting.

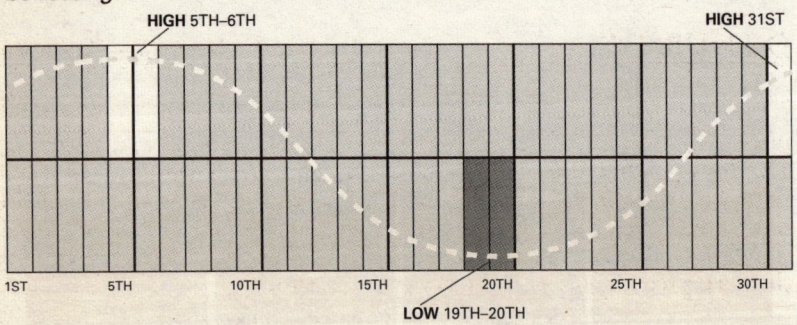

HIGH 5TH–6TH   **HIGH** 31ST

1ST   5TH   10TH   15TH   20TH   25TH   30TH

LOW 19TH–20TH

3 MONDAY
Moon Age Day 6   Moon Sign Sagittarius

am ....

pm...
Even if there is a great deal going on around you today, you may feel
there is not very much happening to you personally. This situation is
influenced by the position of the Moon. You can afford to be patient and
wait a while because the lunar high will soon be around. In the meantime
you can plan and also put the finishing touches to things.

4 TUESDAY
Moon Age Day 7   Moon Sign Sagittarius

am ....

pm...
Relationships could mean a great deal to you at this time, and it's important
to find moments to contemplate what you can do to contribute more to
them. This is especially true in a romantic sense, though you should also
be able to find ways and means to consolidate not only attachments but
also more casual associations.

5 WEDNESDAY
Moon Age Day 8   Moon Sign Capricorn

am ....

pm..
Now you need to get on with things and to take as much positive action
as you can. Trends assist you to get everything working well for you at
the moment. Your great insight into the way others are likely to behave is
highlighted, and you can use it to influence what is going on around you.
Your contributions to life tend to be positive at this time.

6 THURSDAY
Moon Age Day 9   Moon Sign Capricorn

am ....

pm..
The lunar high assists you to think big, and you needn't allow your
thoughts to be high-jacked by those who have less belief than you do
right now. From a financial point of view you should be able to make
significant progress, and can get things well lined up, perhaps more so
than expected. Positivity is the key to success today.

7 FRIDAY
Moon Age Day 10   Moon Sign Aquarius

am ....

pm..
The acquisitive side of your nature is emphasised today, encouraging you to hold on tight to what you believe is yours. This is slightly unfortunate because there are also planetary trends around that suggest the more you share, the more gains you can make. Avoid being too quick to judge others at the moment, and be willing to show your sympathy.

8 SATURDAY
Moon Age Day 11   Moon Sign Aquarius

am ....

pm..
This has potential to be a go-ahead period, especially in terms of the practical aspects of life. You have what it takes to get things falling into place without actually contributing very much. This is really because of what you have done in the past, and the rewards you can achieve now are due to previous hard work. Relationships look better today.

9 SUNDAY
Moon Age Day 12   Moon Sign Aquarius

am ....

pm..
This is a fine time to look at documents and to sign any important papers that you have been mulling over for a while. Your mind is astute and you can use this trait to avoid getting yourself into any situation you will regret later. Be prepared for elements of the past to play a part in your thinking today, especially in terms of love and affection.

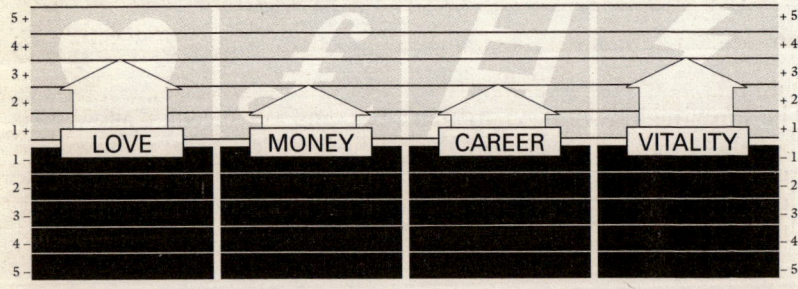

10 MONDAY

Moon Age Day 13   Moon Sign Pisces

am ....

pm...
Today marks one of those times when it really pays to be assertive and to put your point of view across somewhat forcefully. Of course you won't want to upset others, but you can convince them to respond positively if you put your cards on the table. Opportunities to take a journey or a holiday should be carefully considered.

11 TUESDAY

Moon Age Day 14   Moon Sign Pisces

am ....

pm...
Professionally speaking there are still some positive trends around and this is certainly the month to get ahead if you have the chance. Some Capricorn people may even be thinking about a total change of career or embarking on some new learning process to help things along. You have rarely been as progressive as you can be now.

12 WEDNESDAY

Moon Age Day 15   Moon Sign Aries

am ....

pm...
Mars is in your solar eighth house at the moment and so it would be sensible to put aside a few hours to sort out the wheat from the chaff. Not everything around you at the moment is very useful, and there are some elements of life you may see as being totally redundant. Without being brutal, you need to do something about this.

13 THURSDAY

Moon Age Day 16   Moon Sign Aries

am ....

pm...
There might be little time for fun or relaxation today, particularly if you are busy in other ways. Be prepared to act if you need to put some plans for enjoyment on hold. That doesn't mean you can't enjoy the day, merely that you are encouraged to focus on practical things. By the evening you should be in a better position to socialise.

14 FRIDAY
Moon Age Day 17   Moon Sign Taurus

am ....

pm ....
Mercury brings a trend that allows you to work positively towards your objectives, and probably quite quickly too. The little planet enhances your communication skills and assists your attempts to tackle any matters you have been ignoring over recent days. With a greater degree of personal confidence, anything is possible.

15 SATURDAY
Moon Age Day 18   Moon Sign Taurus

am ....

pm ....
You should now be able to capitalise on a fairly hectic social scene, and this will help you to make life more interesting and fulfilling in a general sense. If there hasn't been an opportunity to tell your partner or lover how you feel about them, now would be an excellent time to do so. Any gesture you make should be much appreciated today.

16 SUNDAY
Moon Age Day 19   Moon Sign Gemini

am ....

pm ....
Career issues are likely to be helped by your capacity for hard work. This may not seem to be the most positive trend to be experiencing on a Sunday, but even if you don't have to go to work today, you have scope to come up with some amazing ideas, which you can put into practice tomorrow. Why not take time out to enjoy yourself later?

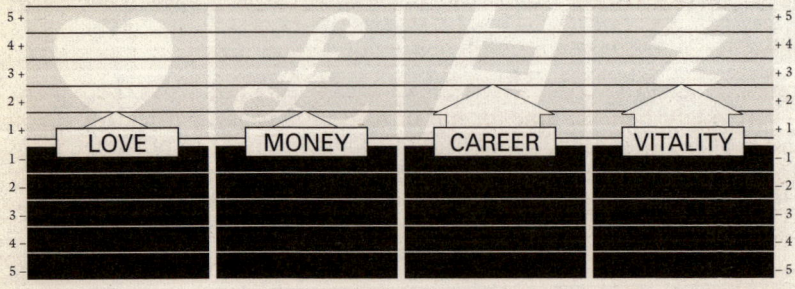

17 MONDAY
Moon Age Day 20   Moon Sign Gemini

am ....

pm ....
Your career can benefit from a massive boost with the Sun in your solar tenth house. It pays to take advantage of changing circumstances and to make sure you don't miss any chance to do those things you instinctively know are going to help you along. Patience is a given as far as Capricorn is concerned, and allied to effort it is a powerful weapon.

18 TUESDAY
Moon Age Day 21   Moon Sign Gemini

am ....

pm ....
Keep looking and listening because there are opportunities for gain today that you might not have expected. You won't find a lot of what you need written on any wall today, and it's true that you might have to search to find the incentives you require. However, this is half the fun and your curiosity is likely to be emphasised right now.

19 WEDNESDAY
Moon Age Day 22   Moon Sign Cancer

am ....

pm ....
A sense of frustration is a natural aspect of life at this time, and you can thank the lunar low for the fact. It would now be less sensible to act on impulse and much better to look at everything in your careful Capricorn way in order to avoid getting into a muddle. Not only can you help yourself, but you can give others a hand too.

20 THURSDAY
Moon Age Day 23   Moon Sign Cancer

am ....

pm ....
If things suddenly stall, it is probably for a reason, and it's worth finding out what that might be. It's true that you may not be pushing over any buses today, but you should suffer less from the lunar low than many people do, simply because you are as happy plodding along as you are in any race. Beware of taking chance remarks seriously.

21 FRIDAY

Moon Age Day 24   Moon Sign Leo

am ....

pm..

There can be certain pressures building up in your life today – or at any rate that is the way it might appear to be at first sight. Your organisational skills are so well honed that you can turn almost any vice into a virtue while the Sun occupies its present position. On the way you are perfectly placed to be of great use to those around you.

22 SATURDAY

Moon Age Day 25   Moon Sign Leo

am ....

pm..

Common sense plus practical ability is a great combination. Some of the less favourable short-term aspects of the last few days are now moving away, allowing you to feel less cluttered and more positive about life. Getting involved in any situations that you suspect could be a disaster is not to be recommended just now.

23 SUNDAY

Moon Age Day 26   Moon Sign Virgo

am ....

pm..

What happens today should assist you to broaden your horizons and offer you new incentives on more than one level. The Sun is now moving into your solar eleventh house, giving you an opportunity to mix with a wider social circle, and encouraging you to forge links with people who could, in the fullness of time, become trusted and valued friends.

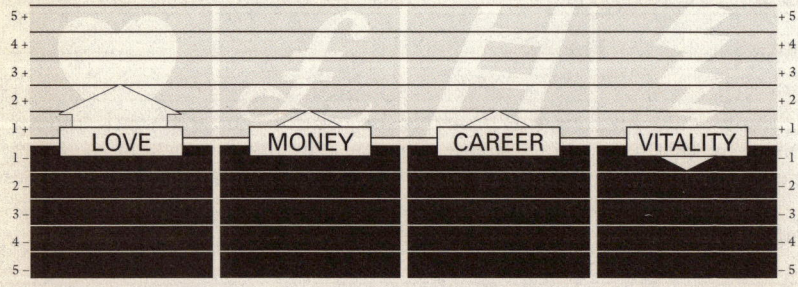

24 MONDAY
Moon Age Day 27   Moon Sign Virgo

am ....

pm...
A new week dawns, and this is a time during which your love life and relationships could help you to put a very definite smile on your face. If you don't have the time to do everything you wish in a practical sense, be willing to leave some of it for another day. You can persuade most of the people you meet today to be reasonable.

25 TUESDAY
Moon Age Day 28   Moon Sign Libra

am ....

pm...
A good sense of organisation is important now. Work and practical affairs offer you scope to keep yourself generally busy today, together with the comfort of knowing that life is running in a smooth and steady way. Even if excitement is difficult to find, you needn't be fazed by that fact at the moment.

26 WEDNESDAY
Moon Age Day 29   Moon Sign Libra

am ....

pm...
It's worth being a little more adventurous now, particularly in terms of finding ways to improve your present financial status, no matter how much you have to chance your arm to do so. If you are feeling confident in your own abilities and forward planning, you can afford to take the sort of calculated risk that you might normally leave well alone.

27 THURSDAY
Moon Age Day 0   Moon Sign Scorpio

am ....

pm...
Don't be too keen to work. Getting out and about, away from routines, does wonders for your attitude at present. Outdoor pursuits should suit you fine, and you needn't worry too much about what the weather decides to do. If circumstances keep you rooted to the spot, you will need to turn up the level of your imagination instead.

28 FRIDAY
Moon Age Day 1   Moon Sign Scorpio

am ....

pm..
You may feel that it is time to concentrate on life's material necessities, which include money. Even if you know how to make it at present, perhaps unfortunately you might also have a pretty good idea as to how to spend it! Keeping your purse or wallet firmly closed would be your best option, but how likely is that?

29 SATURDAY
Moon Age Day 2   Moon Sign Sagittarius

am ....

pm..
Happiness is there for the taking, and good times in relationships allow you to create a weekend that is safe, warm and generally comfortable. Although you can't count on the support of everyone you know, in the main the people you rely on the most come up trumps on your behalf. Concentrate on issues that can make you better off financially.

30 SUNDAY
Moon Age Day 3   Moon Sign Sagittarius

am ....

pm..
It's almost certain that today will be a mixed bag, though you can still make positive progress in a general sense. If there are any frustrations, these could well come about as a result of the attitude of colleagues, particularly those who are ploughing a very different furrow to your own. It pays to keep abreast of what is happening in your immediate locality.

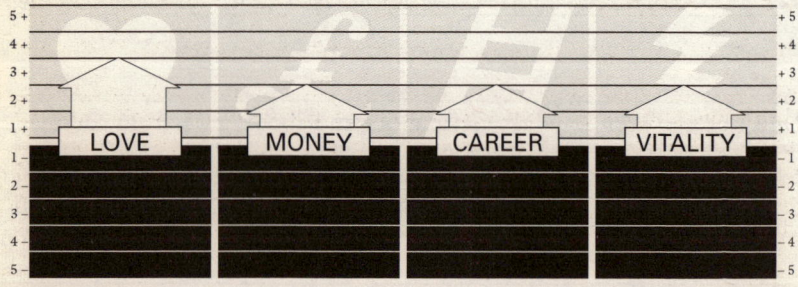

31 MONDAY   *Moon Age Day 4   Moon Sign Capricorn*

am ....

pm..

It would benefit you to get an early start today and to realise, right from the word go, that fortune now favours the brave. The lunar high offers you the chance to shine, and should lift your spirits considerably, bearing in mind the way you might have been thinking and acting across the last few days. Be prepared to take the odd chance.

1 TUESDAY   *Moon Age Day 5   Moon Sign Capricorn*

am ....

pm..

It's time to come out of the corner, if that's where you feel you have been for a while, and to really show the world what you can do. Today is all about demonstrating to others what you are capable of achieving, and proving something to yourself on the way as well. Look out for opportunities to make financial gains.

2 WEDNESDAY   *Moon Age Day 6   Moon Sign Aquarius*

am ....

pm..

Your social life should now be mentally uplifting, particularly if you are mixing with some extremely interesting people. There are those you know, together with the individuals who you are welcoming new into your life at this time. No new relationship is wasted, and you have scope to look at the world with a great sense of curiosity.

3 THURSDAY   *Moon Age Day 7   Moon Sign Aquarius*

am ....

pm..

Minor disruptions to domestic peace and harmony typify the sort of astrological trends that stand around you right now. Your best approach is to try not to get more involved in them than is strictly necessary, and to stay away from other people's rows. You need peace and quiet, though whether you can find it today remains to be seen.

4 FRIDAY

Moon Age Day 8   Moon Sign Aquarius

am ....

pm..
The Sun – in its present position and with attendant aspects – favours twosomes of all kinds. It doesn't matter whether it's a case of love at first sight, or a business relationship. The fact is that you can find happiness in the company of someone else. Your powers of communication are enhanced and you have much to say for yourself.

5 SATURDAY

Moon Age Day 9   Moon Sign Pisces

am ....

pm..
You can use whatever is happening today to help you feel a good deal more secure, which is never a bad state of affairs for Capricorn. Although you may appear to be conforming to expectations, in reality things could be quite different. The slightly rebellious side of your nature is at work, though like the frantic legs of a swan it is all below the surface.

6 SUNDAY

Moon Age Day 10   Moon Sign Pisces

am ....

pm..
Stand by to make this a 'happening' Sunday. Your intuition is highlighted and should not be ignored. This trait can help you decide whether those who are in the know are being straight with you or not. Rewards can be gleaned from some fairly unexpected places, and may have a bearing on deeper, more personal relationships later in the day.

	LOVE	MONEY	CAREER	VITALITY

November

2011

YOUR MONTH AT A GLANCE

⊕ = Opportunities are around   ⊖ = Be on the defensive   ⬤ = Life is pretty ordinary

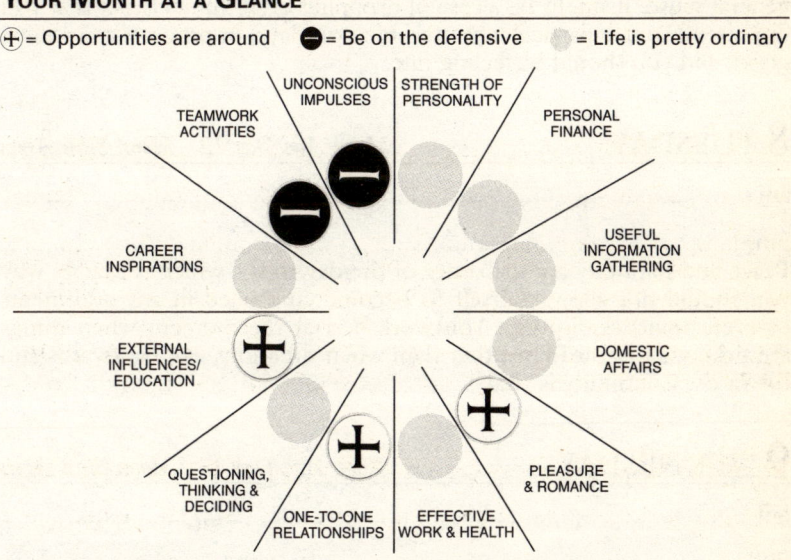

- TEAMWORK ACTIVITIES
- UNCONSCIOUS IMPULSES
- STRENGTH OF PERSONALITY
- PERSONAL FINANCE
- CAREER INSPIRATIONS
- USEFUL INFORMATION GATHERING
- EXTERNAL INFLUENCES/EDUCATION
- DOMESTIC AFFAIRS
- QUESTIONING, THINKING & DECIDING
- ONE-TO-ONE RELATIONSHIPS
- EFFECTIVE WORK & HEALTH
- PLEASURE & ROMANCE

NOVEMBER HIGHS AND LOWS

Here I show you how the rhythms of the Moon will affect you this month. Like the tide, your energies and abilities will rise and fall with its pattern. When it is above the centre line, go for it, when it is below, you should be resting.

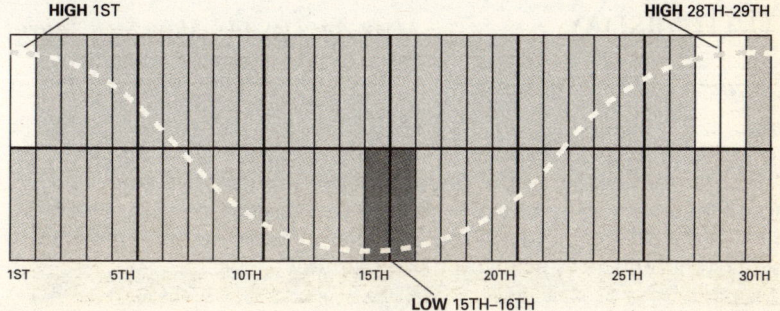

HIGH 1ST   HIGH 28TH–29TH

1ST   5TH   10TH   15TH   20TH   25TH   30TH

LOW 15TH–16TH

7 MONDAY
Moon Age Day 11   Moon Sign Aries

am ....

pm...
Be prepared to respond to minor delays and difficulties that come along today. You needn't let these prevent you from moving forward in a general sense. It might be a case of dropping everything else so that you can attend to one particular matter, but your level of progress can still be good, and you should be feeling fine.

8 TUESDAY
Moon Age Day 12   Moon Sign Aries

am ....

pm...
Peace and harmony are the order of the day today, which is exactly why you should not allow yourself to become embroiled in any arguments or even pointless disputes. You work best at the moment when things are ticking along steadily rather than when situations jerk backwards and forwards. Continuity is vital.

9 WEDNESDAY
Moon Age Day 13   Moon Sign Aries

am ....

pm...
A slight decline in ambition and drive is now indicated. This is because you have more than one planet in your solar twelfth house for the moment, supporting a quieter phase and a tendency to allow others to do some of the planning and the work. There's nothing wrong with that, because it avoids you taking too much on your own shoulders.

10 THURSDAY
Moon Age Day 14   Moon Sign Taurus

am ....

pm...
Now you can reap the benefits of more beneficial social trends, and even if you are not making all the running in practical areas of your life, you should be quite willing to get together with like-minded people in order to talk things through. Much can be achieved by saying the right things, and current influences help you to do that now.

11 FRIDAY
Moon Age Day 15   Moon Sign Taurus

am ....

pm...
Relating to others is still favoured, this time by the Moon. This is especially true where romance is concerned, and you can certainly show the deeply affectionate side of Capricorn at this stage of the year. New opportunities could well be available in this particular area of your life, though ordinary friendship also offers rewards.

12 SATURDAY
Moon Age Day 16   Moon Sign Gemini

am ....

pm...
There are inauspicious trends associated with travel around now. This doesn't mean you should avoid moving around, simply that you would be wise to exercise a little more care. Hastily conceived schemes are best avoided if at all possible, in favour of following ideas and plans that were laid down quite some time ago.

13 SUNDAY
Moon Age Day 17   Moon Sign Gemini

am ....

pm...
A day to stand back and take another look at vital situations. You need to ask yourself whether you are really seeing arguments from all sides and taking all important factors into account. As a rule you are a very astute person, but some of this ability is missing for a few days. You might even decide to seek the advice of someone close to you.

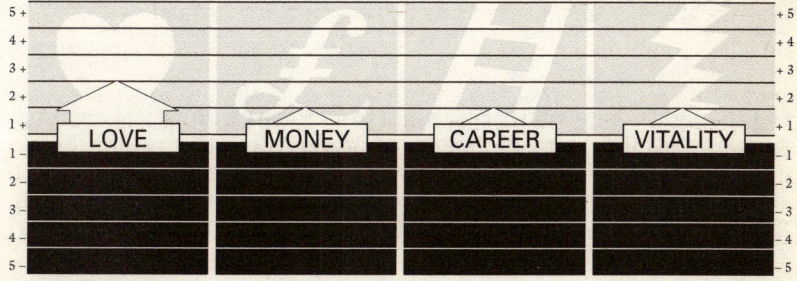

14 MONDAY   *Moon Age Day 18   Moon Sign Gemini*

am ....

pm...
Constant attention to detail is so much a part of your nature that you might not even realise you are doing it. However, right now you are encouraged to take a rather more vague approach than usual and possibly even to leave certain things to chance. It isn't what you are usually about, but as a temporary strategy it may work better than you imagine.

15 TUESDAY   *Moon Age Day 19   Moon Sign Cancer*

am ....

pm...
You may now have to deal with an almost total standstill when it comes to getting on in life generally. This is the influence of the lunar low, though there shouldn't be anything especially troubling about the situation. It pays to take things steadily for a day or two, and that shouldn't really matter. It's an ideal time to meditate and to take stock.

16 WEDNESDAY   *Moon Age Day 20   Moon Sign Cancer*

am ....

pm...
Personality issues could now get in the way of advancement, particularly if what other people think about you is not the impression you are trying to give. There is always a chance that you are putting in too much effort in certain directions, which can lead to disappointment and fatigue. Why not let life simply wash over you for a while?

17 THURSDAY   *Moon Age Day 21   Moon Sign Leo*

am ....

pm...
The spotlight is now on specific issues from the past. Powerful emotions swirl around, thanks to the influence of Venus in your twelfth house, and you need to be prepared to at least appear to lose some battles. If something doesn't really matter to you, don't spend hours defending it. This is a waste of time and energy that you really don't need.

18 FRIDAY
Moon Age Day 22   Moon Sign Leo

am ....

pm..
This would be an ideal time to make contact with old faces and also to encourage new friendships to develop from what were originally just loose attachments. It takes a lot for you to make a really good friend, so they come along quite rarely. Present trends create the sort of furnace in which long-lasting commitments can be forged.

19 SATURDAY
Moon Age Day 23   Moon Sign Virgo

am ....

pm..
You have what it takes to articulate your ideas very well this weekend, and you also have access to a great deal of ingenuity, which you can plough into new situations. The people around you at the moment can be either a help or a hindrance, depending on the situation. You can only judge things as and when they arise.

20 SUNDAY
Moon Age Day 24   Moon Sign Virgo

am ....

pm..
Even if you seem to have less scope to influence certain people today than you did yesterday, you needn't become depressed or demoralised as a result. On the contrary, the more you try right now, the greater the gains are likely to be. It isn't like Capricorn to fall at the first fence – or any fence at all!

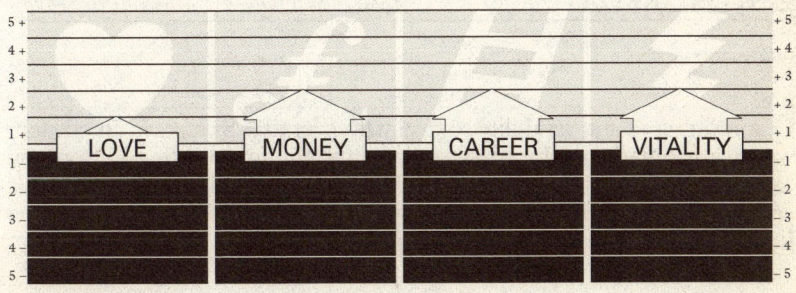

21 MONDAY
Moon Age Day 25   Moon Sign Virgo

am ....

pm..
Today's influences could so easily support changes you wish to make in your career, or even a change of job in some cases. There could well be a lot going on around you in the professional sphere, but there is no indication that these things are taking place against your best interests. You remain quite shrewd and well able to cope.

22 TUESDAY
Moon Age Day 26   Moon Sign Libra

am ....

pm..
Commitments undertaken at this time could end up lasting much longer than you expected, but once again there is nothing difficult or malicious about the planetary trends that surround you at this time. On the contrary, you are still in a position to get most things working out more or less exactly as you would wish.

23 WEDNESDAY
Moon Age Day 27   Moon Sign Libra

am ....

pm..
Make the most of any chances to reward your ego at this time. Some of your efforts from the past could now begin to pay significant dividends, perhaps much earlier than you expected. There isn't much doubt about the fact that you are on the ball in all mental exercises, and you can come up trumps when it comes to organising money.

24 THURSDAY ☿
Moon Age Day 28   Moon Sign Scorpio

am ....

pm..
Common sense and an ability to deal with everyday matters in an efficient way are hallmarks of the present planetary alignments. In addition you can make full use of your great intuition in assessing the natures of people you have to deal with at this time, and this can be an invaluable tool on the path towards greater achievements.

25 FRIDAY ☿ *Moon Age Day 0   Moon Sign Scorpio*

am ....

pm...
Your social life can be given a boost, thanks to the position of Mars, which is now in your solar ninth house. Be open to new ideas and stay on the right side of people you instinctively know can work alongside you towards your best interests. Shared goals and common ideals are typical of what the planets are offering now.

26 SATURDAY ☿ *Moon Age Day 1   Moon Sign Sagittarius*

am ....

pm...
You would be wise to exercise caution this weekend in terms of what you commit yourself to doing. It would be so easy at present to get carried away by things, and often without realising. In some cases this is fine because you need variety in your life. What doesn't work is being forced into some sort of corner.

27 SUNDAY ☿ *Moon Age Day 2   Moon Sign Sagittarius*

am ....

pm...
Stand by to make the most of a potentially quieter day, or at least one that offers you more time to think, with less pressure being placed upon you. This is a temporary lull because the lunar high is on its way, offering all the excitement and incentives you could need. A stay-at-home sort of day would be no bad thing for Capricorn now.

LOVE	MONEY	CAREER	VITALITY

28 MONDAY ☿ *Moon Age Day 3 Moon Sign Capricorn*

am ....

pm...

It's time to whip up enthusiasm and self-belief in bucket-loads. Today offers you the chance to get down to what really needs doing, and on the way to sort out anyone who requires assistance. It's the start of a new week, and one that encourages much in the way of independent thinking and positive actions undertaken with confidence.

29 TUESDAY ☿ *Moon Age Day 4 Moon Sign Capricorn*

am ....

pm...

The lunar high supports sudden changes in direction and even planned alterations to your course. Take advantage of this interlude and use it to the best of your ability in order to make the progress you are seeking, especially in a material sense. There may be little time for nostalgia right now, and you should be willing to make sacrifices if necessary.

30 WEDNESDAY ☿ *Moon Age Day 5 Moon Sign Aquarius*

am ....

pm...

Stay clear of disagreements today if you can possibly manage to do so. You may decide it would be better not to interact too much with people at all, rather than to become involved in pointless rows. Such a state of affairs is far less likely in terms of deep attachments. Capricorn subjects who are looking for love can make progress now.

1 THURSDAY ☿ *Moon Age Day 6 Moon Sign Aquarius*

am ....

pm...

Even if you feel quite pressured on a practical level, this shouldn't prevent you from getting on well all the same. At this stage of the week, and in the midst of some demanding situations, certain people would buckle with the pressure. You, fortunately, are not one of them. Your strength lies in your willingness to give support when you can.

2 FRIDAY ☿ *Moon Age Day 7   Moon Sign Pisces*

am..

pm..
Independence counts, and if there are specific tasks to be completed
today, it's natural to want to do everything your own way. That's fine, just
as long as you can persuade others that you know what you are talking
about. Be prepared to work hard to get your message across, especially to
any particularly awkward types.

3 SATURDAY ☿ *Moon Age Day 8   Moon Sign Pisces*

am..

pm..
Capitalise on a high point in your love life today. Single Capricorn
subjects have scope to attract a good deal of attention, whilst those
involved in settled relationships can achieve an even better understanding
and contentment. Practical progress could be slightly restricted, but if
you are busy in other ways, this shouldn't matter.

4 SUNDAY ☿ *Moon Age Day 9   Moon Sign Pisces*

am..

pm..
The spotlight is now on your determination to get down to the real nitty-
gritty of issues. Beware of being side-tracked, and make sure that others
are telling the truth. How can you be certain? Well, at the moment all you
have to do is to turn your intuition up to full. Few people would manage
to pull the wool over your eyes at this time.

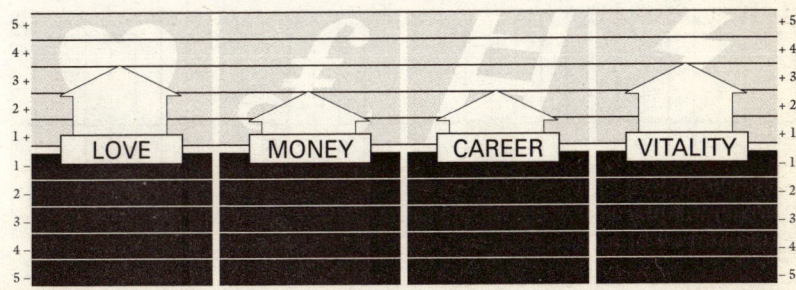

♈

December

2011

YOUR MONTH AT A GLANCE

⊕ = Opportunities are around   ⦸ = Be on the defensive   = Life is pretty ordinary

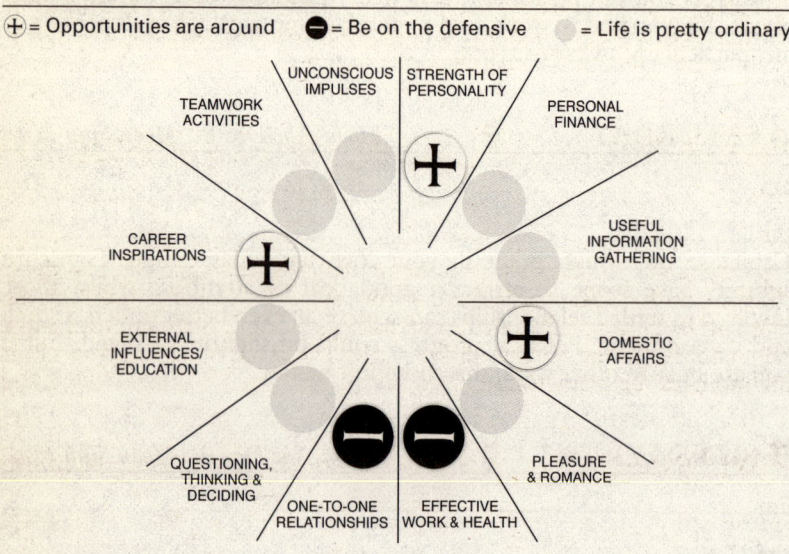

TEAMWORK ACTIVITIES

UNCONSCIOUS IMPULSES

STRENGTH OF PERSONALITY

PERSONAL FINANCE

CAREER INSPIRATIONS ⊕

⊕ USEFUL INFORMATION GATHERING

EXTERNAL INFLUENCES/ EDUCATION

⊕ DOMESTIC AFFAIRS

QUESTIONING, THINKING & DECIDING

ONE-TO-ONE RELATIONSHIPS ⦸

⦸ EFFECTIVE WORK & HEALTH

PLEASURE & ROMANCE

DECEMBER HIGHS AND LOWS

Here I show you how the rhythms of the Moon will affect you this month. Like the tide, your energies and abilities will rise and fall with its pattern. When it is above the centre line, go for it, when it is below, you should be resting.

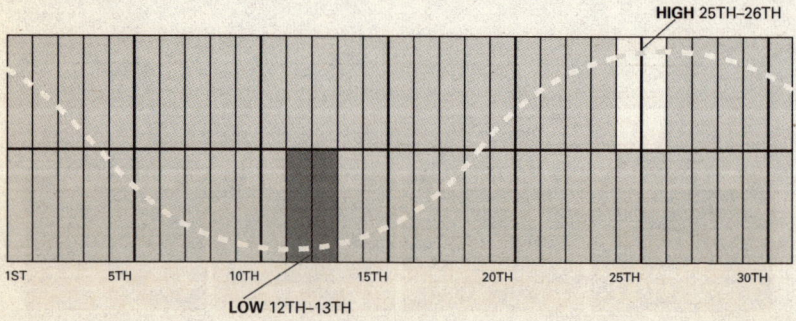

HIGH 25TH–26TH

1ST   5TH   10TH   15TH   20TH   25TH   30TH

LOW 12TH–13TH

5 MONDAY ☿ *Moon Age Day 10   Moon Sign Aries*

am ....

pm..

At home you should be particularly tuned in to your own feelings today, and this should assist you to find more time to talk to the people you care about the most. You have what it takes to attract solid support from your partner or other family members, and even if you are busy practically, it is likely to be domestic life that matters the most.

6 TUESDAY ☿ *Moon Age Day 11   Moon Sign Aries*

am ....

pm..

Unnecessary arguments are a distinct possibility today, and the best thing you can do is to stay away from them. You won't help yourself at the moment by getting embroiled in situations you can't really control, and a calm and steady approach to life works best. Instead of having your say at the moment, be ready to listen.

7 WEDNESDAY ☿ *Moon Age Day 12   Moon Sign Taurus*

am ....

pm..

There are good reasons to seek out some entertaining experiences at this stage in December. It might only just have occurred to you that Christmas is only a couple of weeks away, so you need to think about any arranging there is to do. A chance meeting at some point today could lead to a pleasant surprise and an enjoyable interlude.

8 THURSDAY ☿ *Moon Age Day 13   Moon Sign Taurus*

am ....

pm..

The emphasis on love and romance remains. Venus is now in your solar first house and there is hardly a better planetary position than this for allowing relationships to find their own positive level. Make sure that the things you say to others have a genuine softness to them, and that you show your most appealing side.

9 FRIDAY ☿ *Moon Age Day 14   Moon Sign Taurus*

am ....

pm..
You might decide it's necessary to get down to brass tacks today, even if you would prefer not to do so in many respects. Unpleasantness is something you would much rather avoid, but if you want life to turn out the way you think it should you will have to take a stand. You now have scope to get closer to something very important.

10 SATURDAY ☿ *Moon Age Day 15   Moon Sign Gemini*

am ....

pm..
Take the opportunity to seek out the wide blue yonder. Even though the chill winds of winter are starting to blow, being out of doors can work wonders. A shopping trip would be no bad thing today, though it's worth remembering that the first thing you see may not be the bargain you are looking for. Be prepared to keep searching.

11 SUNDAY ☿ *Moon Age Day 16   Moon Sign Gemini*

am ....

pm..
This would be an ideal period to reassess certain matters, since it offers you a second chance to get a particular issue right. This is quite fortunate because it allows you to polish something until in shines, which is what Capricorn loves to do. In any situation today you certainly needn't be last in the queue, and should be up for a challenge.

	LOVE	MONEY	CAREER	VITALITY

12 MONDAY   ☿   *Moon Age Day 17   Moon Sign Cancer*

am ....

pm...
The time is now right to take a break. Fortunately for you the lunar low comes along quite early in the month, and that means it will be well out of the way before the build-up to the festive season really gets started. You can afford to let others take the strain while you spend a few hours thinking, a necessary prerequisite for even the busiest Capricorn.

13 TUESDAY   ☿   *Moon Age Day 18   Moon Sign Cancer*

am ....

pm...
Taking risks is to be avoided today, and you should also think carefully before making any rash spending decisions. If you are expected to do some sort of deal today, your interests are best served by either deferring it or making certain that you have everything sorted in your mind. Serenity is the key this evening.

14 WEDNESDAY   ☿   *Moon Age Day 19   Moon Sign Leo*

am ....

pm...
It's important not to allow any self-righteous views to get in the way in significant discussions now. In all truth you should avoid getting embroiled in any difficult situations for the moment. If you keep life light and airy you should get on much better than you would if you begin to take matters far too seriously for your own good.

15 THURSDAY   *Moon Age Day 20   Moon Sign Leo*

am ....

pm...
The Sun is still in your solar twelfth house, where it remains for another few days. This supports an element of withdrawal, so you may not be up for all the hype ahead of the Christmas period. Of course, you can still enjoy the festivities when they arrive, but there is nothing wrong with letting others sort out all the details.

16 FRIDAY

Moon Age Day 21   Moon Sign Leo

am ....

pm ....
Seek out the novel and the unusual if you can because this is a time when you should at least be thinking about broadening your horizons. You presently get the most from life with a combination of quiet observation, followed by quite definite action. Getting to know others is sometimes difficult, though you can soon change that state of affairs.

17 SATURDAY

Moon Age Day 22   Moon Sign Virgo

am ....

pm ....
The spotlight is now on how popular and attractive you are when viewed by others. Stand by for a couple of false starts today, or you may get going, only to find that other people have a very different idea. It won't be many days before the Sun crosses into your solar first house, and then you can make sure that the fun really begins!

18 SUNDAY

Moon Age Day 23   Moon Sign Virgo

am ....

pm ....
Trends highlight your great desire to do your own thing, even at the expense of those around you. This is something that might be quite difficult to avoid, but it's only a short interlude. You won't do yourself any harm at all by standing up for your rights, especially against some sort of authority figure. There is satisfaction to be had.

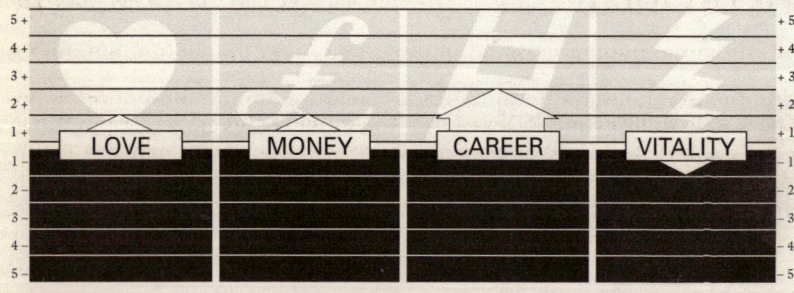

19 MONDAY
Moon Age Day 24   Moon Sign Libra

am ....

pm..
Be prepared to deal with a day of very busy demands when it might be hard to get everything done that you want to finish. There is much to be said for watching and waiting in some situations, or relying on the positive advice of friends. The busiest time of December is not far away, and you should be winding up to something important.

20 TUESDAY
Moon Age Day 25   Moon Sign Libra

am ....

pm..
What an excellent day this would be to get yourself in the thick of things. That first-house Venus can be especially potent right now, encouraging you to get to know more people and to put across your point of view in a very positive way. After a less than sparkling start to December you can really begin to get things going now.

21 WEDNESDAY
Moon Age Day 26   Moon Sign Scorpio

am ....

pm..
Your focus now should be on communication, even if things in this area don't turn out entirely as you would expect. Little Mercury remains in your solar twelfth house for a few days more, supporting a feeling of restriction when it comes to talking to others. This is particularly the case for those you don't know very well.

22 THURSDAY
Moon Age Day 27   Moon Sign Scorpio

am ....

pm..
Venus is now moving on ahead of the Sun, and into your solar second house. This is a very positive position for money matters, and you could well be somehow better off at this stage than you expected. Why not use at least part of today to finalise those last-minute details and to wrap any presents that are still lying in the cupboard?

23 FRIDAY
Moon Age Day 28   Moon Sign Sagittarius

am...

pm...
It won't be long before the lunar high, which this year coincides with Christmas itself. However, for now you can afford to be slightly quieter, a bit more reserved and more inclined to watch than to take part. There is nothing wrong with letting others make the running while you simply show how warm, approachable and sincere you can be.

24 SATURDAY
Moon Age Day 29   Moon Sign Sagittarius

am...

pm...
It's sometimes good to stand back and watch something that usually has people running around from pillar to post. Christmas Eve could well offer you just such an opportunity. You are in a position to take things a little easier than would generally be the case, particularly if you are confident that everything will turn out fine in the end.

25 SUNDAY
Moon Age Day 0   Moon Sign Capricorn

am...

pm...
Everything comes together for Christmas Day as far as you are concerned. The lunar high is here and the Sun is now in your solar first house. Decisive action is indicated, and if you don't manage to make yourself the life and soul of any Christmas party, something is radically amiss. A day to join in with festivities on all sides and also to travel if you can.

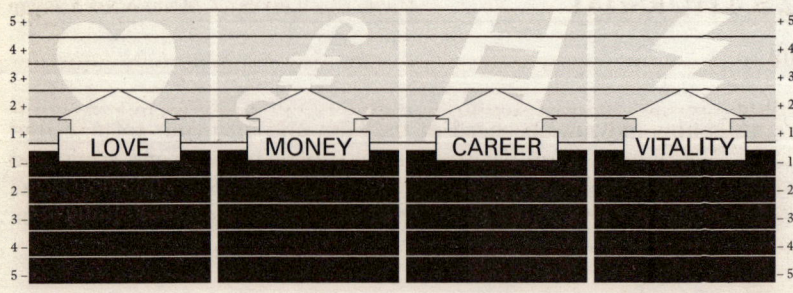

26 MONDAY
Moon Age Day 1   Moon Sign Capricorn

am ....

pm..

Things can continue to be hectic but good fun. You needn't have much truck with rules and regulations today, even those set down by family members, and you might decide to be something of an anarchist for the moment. Still, it's time to show your impish sense of humour and your determination to get everyone joining in.

27 TUESDAY
Moon Age Day 2   Moon Sign Aquarius

am ....

pm..

An element of restlessness is indicated today, though it might be difficult for you to identify exactly why this state of affairs has come about. You can blame the position of the Moon, but that is no excuse for not treating others properly. The best way of banishing strange thoughts is to concentrate instead on the lives of those around you.

28 WEDNESDAY
Moon Age Day 3   Moon Sign Aquarius

am ....

pm..

The emphasis is now on your desire to complete a particular project and your determination not to allow anything to get in your way. Is this something you should have done days or weeks ago? You need to ask yourself whether today is really the right time to address it. Why not put it on the shelf until after the New Year and go on having fun?

29 THURSDAY
Moon Age Day 4   Moon Sign Pisces

am ....

pm..

Your mind could now be working overtime. Love affairs are favoured today, and travel is also well marked, particularly if you are planning to visit people you haven't spent time with for a while. No one likes to feel bullied into doing things that go against the grain, though you could be quite surprised in the end. It's worth putting yourself out.

30 FRIDAY
Moon Age Day 5   Moon Sign Pisces

am...

pm...
The time is right for establishing good relations with just about anyone, even people who have not been your favourites in the past. You have a good chance to get others to take you more seriously now, and you might be able to attract, as a friend, someone who wasn't very kind to you in years gone by. It's time to forgive and forget.

31 SATURDAY
Moon Age Day 6   Moon Sign Pisces

am...

pm...
It seems as though enthusiasm remains at a peak and this is certainly no bad way to end a year. Your best approach today is to concentrate on having fun, and on making it possible for those around you to have a good time too. New Year's resolutions can be put on hold, because the enjoyment is hardly likely to stop at midnight!

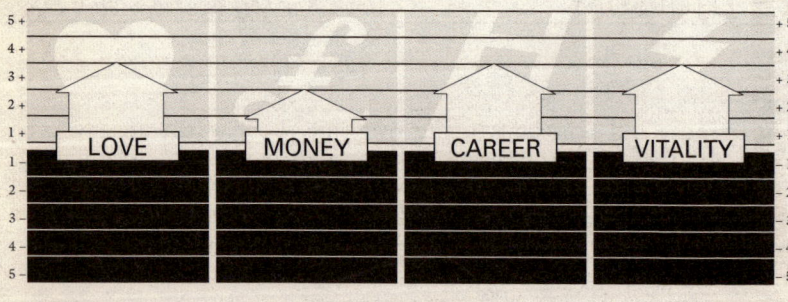

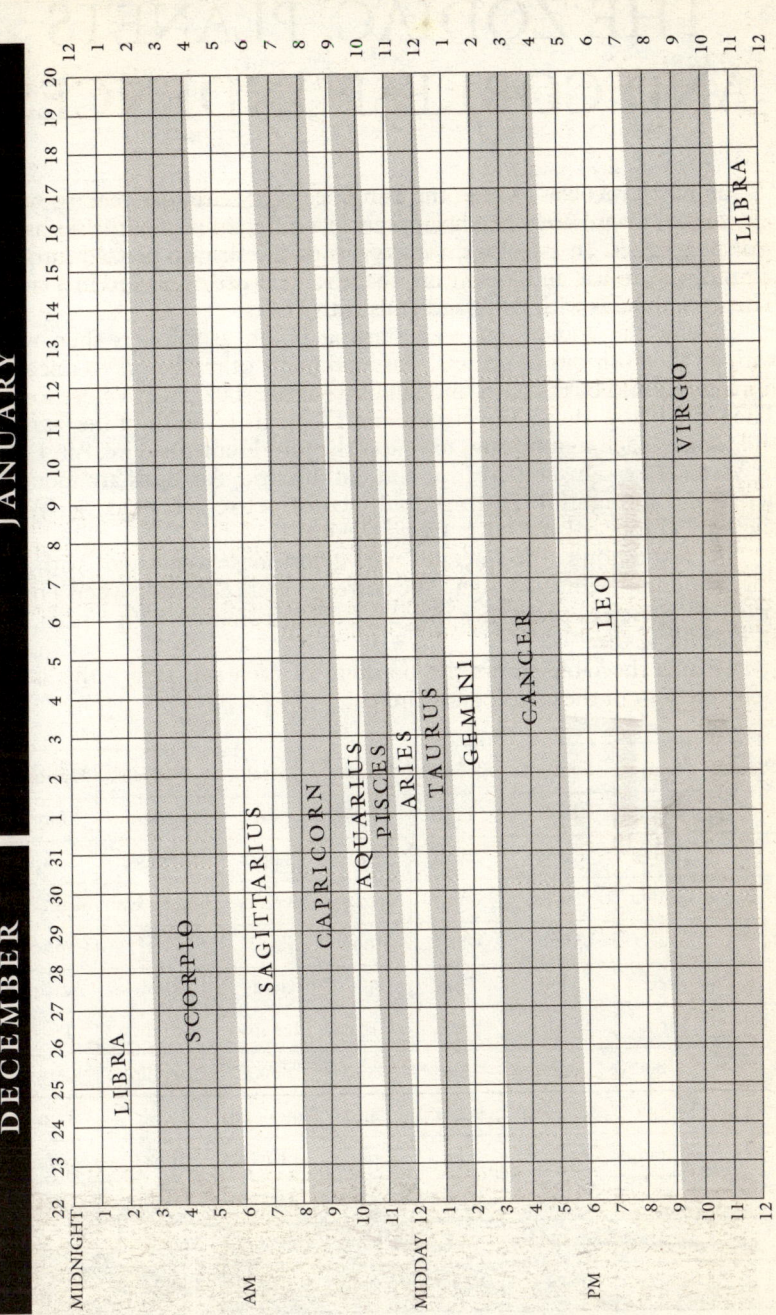

THE ZODIAC, PLANETS AND CORRESPONDENCES

The Earth revolves around the Sun once every calendar year, so when viewed from Earth the Sun appears in a different part of the sky as the year progresses. In astrology, these parts of the sky are divided into the signs of the zodiac and this means that the signs are organised in a circle. The circle begins with Aries and ends with Pisces.

Taking the zodiac sign as a starting point, astrologers then work with all the positions of planets, stars and many other factors to calculate horoscopes and birth charts and tell us what the stars have in store for us. The table below shows the planets and Elements for each of the signs of the zodiac. Each sign belongs to one of the four Elements: Fire, Air, Earth or Water. Fire signs are creative and enthusiastic; Air signs are mentally active and thoughtful; Earth signs are constructive and practical; Water signs are emotional and have strong feelings.

It also shows the metals and gemstones associated with, or corresponding with, each sign. The correspondence is made when a metal or stone possesses properties that are held in common with a particular sign of the zodiac.

Finally, the table shows the opposite of each star sign – this is the opposite sign in the astrological circle.

Placed	Sign	Symbol	Element	Planet	Metal	Stone	Opposite
1	Aries	Ram	Fire	Mars	Iron	Bloodstone	Libra
2	Taurus	Bull	Earth	Venus	Copper	Sapphire	Scorpio
3	Gemini	Twins	Air	Mercury	Mercury	Tiger's Eye	Sagittarius
4	Cancer	Crab	Water	Moon	Silver	Pearl	Capricorn
5	Leo	Lion	Fire	Sun	Gold	Ruby	Aquarius
6	Virgo	Maiden	Earth	Mercury	Mercury	Sardonyx	Pisces
7	Libra	Scales	Air	Venus	Copper	Sapphire	Aries
8	Scorpio	Scorpion	Water	Pluto	Plutonium	Jasper	Taurus
9	Sagittarius	Archer	Fire	Jupiter	Tin	Topaz	Gemini
10	Capricorn	Goat	Earth	Saturn	Lead	Black Onyx	Cancer
11	Aquarius	Waterbearer	Air	Uranus	Uranium	Amethyst	Leo
12	Pisces	Fishes	Water	Neptune	Tin	Moonstone	Virgo